Merry
Christmas, Baby

Also by PAULA L. WOODS and FELIX H. LIDDELL
I, Too, Sing America
I Hear a Symphony

★

Edited by PAULA L. WOODS
Spooks, Spies, and Private Eyes

Merry Christmas, Baby

A CHRISTMAS and KWANZAA Treasury

Edited by PAULA L. WOODS *and* FELIX H. LIDDELL

HarperCollins*Publishers*

MERRY CHRISTMAS, BABY:
A CHRISTMAS AND KWANZAA TREASURY

HarperCollins books may be purchased for educational, business,
or sales promotional use. For information please write:
Special Markets Department, HarperCollins Publishers, Inc.,
10 East 53rd Street, New York, NY 10022.

FIRST EDITION

Designed by Moira and Company, Chicago, Illinois.

Packaged by Livre Noir, Los Angeles, California

Library of Congress Cataloging-in-Publication Data
Merry Christmas, Baby: A Christmas and Kwanzaa treasury / edited by Paula L.
Woods and Felix H. Liddell. – 1st ed.
p.   cm.
ISBN 0-06-017395-5
1. Christmas – United States.   2. Afro-Americans – Social life and
customs.   3. Kwanzaa.   4. Christmas – United States – Literary
collections.   5. American literature – Afro-American authors.
I. Woods, Paula L.   II. Liddell, Felix H.
GT4986.A1M47   1996
394.2'61 – dc20
96–10707

96 97 98 99 00 NIT 10 9 8 7 6 5 4 3 2 1

★

To Faith,

whose embodiment of the principle of IMANI

has brought us many blessings

★

CONTENTS

ACKNOWLEDGMENTS

The gifts of encouragement and goodwill have meant the most to us in the completion of this book, and for that we must thank all of the contributors, agents, and publishers who gave unstintingly of their time and attention to our efforts. Special thanks also go to: Rev. Brenda Tapia for her introduction to the marvelous Nancy J. Fairley; to Carolyn McDaniel of the Agape Church of Religious Science for her diligence and perseverance; to Victoria Sanders for going the extra mile; to Michele Rubin at Writers House for her efficiency and good humor.

Among the many museums, galleries, and artists who caught the fire of our quest and made it their own we thank: Paula Allen of Amistad Research Center; Jackie Cox Crite of the Allan Rohan Crite House Museum; Courtney deAngelis of the National Museum of American Art; Tina Dunkley of Clark Atlanta University; Mary Lou Hultgren of Hampton University Museum; Alitash Kebede of Alitash Kebede Gallery; June Kelly of June Kelly Gallery; Halley K. Harrisburg of Michael Rosenfeld Gallery; Tammi Lawson of the Schomburg Center for Research in Black Culture; Harvey Lehman of the Museum of African American Art; Ruth Roberts of the Indianapolis Museum of Art; Misty Moye of the Museum of Fine Arts, Houston; Ramon Price of DuSable Museum of African American History; Thurlow Tibbs; Nannette Carter; Albert Chong; Richard Mayhew; Betye Saar; and Deborah Willis.

We are grateful to those who shaped and nurtured this project: Faith Childs, Arlene Stoltz, and Emily Bernard of the Faith Childs Literary Agency. A special thanks goes to our HarperCollins family: Peternelle van Arsdale, our insightful and supportive editor; Kristen Auclair, who kept us on track; Marjorie Shain Horvitz, a truly astute copy editor; and Joseph Montebello, Suzanne Noli, and Susan Kosko for their design and production expertise. And to Wendy Lowitz and Carol Dungan at Moira and Company—thanks for your design wizardry and great good humor.

Last, but not least, are our family and friends who help us keep Christmas and Kwanzaa in our hearts: Bernice Allen; Jimmy and Kathrene Allen; Tina McElroy and Jonée Ansa; Barbara Appleberry; Father Bohler; Minnie Brister; Barbara Carlson; Carole Edwards; John Forté; Bill Green and Chris Spry; Peter Harris; Priscilla Ferguson and Norman "Guy" Jackson; Julie Jordan; Phyllis Jordan; Blanche Richardson; Joyce "Ms. Christmas" Rushing; Kirstin Spiedel; Andrea and Andrew Van Leesten; Paul Verdon and Michael Haight; and Ann Wang.

Merry Christmas, Baby

🖋 Too often the spirit of Christmas is lost in the commercialism of the shopping season. We get caught up in the crazed search for gifts, the bigger the better to show our love for the recipient or our own status as the giver. Yet each year, as images of pink-faced cherubs and Santas commandeer the media, many Americans feel excluded from the holiday festivities. This feeling is particularly acute for African Americans, for whom the song "White Christmas," the film *It's a Wonderful Life,* or a visit to the mall to see Santa has a subliminal message. Despite the fact that the African American presence is so integrally a part of Christmas tradition that the holidays are not complete for many Americans without Nat "King" Cole's rendition of "The Christmas Song," Ella Fitzgerald wondering "What Are You Doing New Year's?" or anything sung by Johnny Mathis, these other images say to us in fundamental ways, "This holiday doesn't include you."

The feelings of alienation are so acute for some of us that the Christmas season loses its appeal entirely. We are left to drift without a spiritual anchor during the holidays, lost in the whirl of eating, drinking, and merrymaking. Millions have found solace in Kwanzaa, a seven-day celebration of black culture and traditions. Established by Malauna Karenga over twenty-five years ago, the holiday's seven principles link us through language and symbolism to Africa and through ceremony and celebration to our history, culture, and each other. And while some honor Kwanzaa to the exclusion of Christmas, African American families are increasingly searching for ways that the principles embodied in both the Christmas and Kwanzaa traditions can help deepen the meaning of our lives and this special season.

It is possible for us all to restore the meaning of these sacred holidays to our lives. We hope that the words and images in *Merry Christmas, Baby* become your family's guide to recapturing the historical sweep and range of feelings that make up the African American experience of Christmas and Kwanzaa. With the wisdom of Howard Thurman to guide us, this book's goal is to give you "the gifts of recollection calling to heart the graces of life."

Harriet Jacobs's poignant remembrances of Johnkannaus and separation from her family set the historical stage as they recall not only the early forms of African American Christmas celebrations, but of the cruelty slavery inflicted on the most joyous of occasions. The early twentieth-century "Christmas gif'" traditions described in Roscoe Conklin Bruce's letter further connect us to earlier traditions of African American celebration that are also contained in the words of Leslie Pinckney Hill, Jessie Fauset, and others writing at the end of the nineteenth and the beginning of the twentieth century. The art of Horace Pippin, William McKnight Farrow, and Edward Webster add their special power to evoke the more innocent feelings of Christmases past.

What is any holiday celebration without food? Certainly in African American culture, remembrances of Christmases past are inextricably connected to the smells and tastes of the season. A quintet of wonderful chefs and cooks, including Patrick Clark of New York's Tavern on the Green and Leah Chase of New Orleans's Dooky Chase Restaurant, bring those memories alive for us all. And if you can resist their recipes that echo our traditional food lore and bring a new twist to some old favorites, then you're not yet "in the spirit" of the season!

Perhaps a contemporary story of love and trust by Valerie Wilson Wesley will put you in the mood. Or Pulitzer Prize–winner Rita Dove's poignant poem on making Christmas gifts for children, an experience we've all either had or been on the receiving end of at some point in our lives. The message in these and other works by Pearl Cleage, Carol Freeman, and Toi Derricotte is not that the season is about spending the money (which can be in short supply in any household), but about holding onto the love.

The holidays for so many can also be a time of mixed emotions, a time when the tinsel and bright lights bring into painful relief the losses we've suffered. Yet to recognize these painful places allows us to release them and embrace the larger meaning of the season. Aleks D. Pate's story of a tense family Christmas, Nelson George's recollection of a niece's health crisis, Mary Carter Smith's homage to a departed son, all give us the opportunity to remember, but not wallow in, those more poignant moments that are part of any holiday celebration.

But the holidays are also about the good times, about laughing until the tears roll down our faces, about tapping our feet to that blues classic "Merry Christmas, Baby." An array of contributors, including Langston Hughes, Nancy J. Fairley, and Daryl Cumber Dance, remind us of the healing power of laughter, especially during the holidays. And if you've forgotten just how awful those holiday letters can be, the Justice family's Christmas greeting may be just what the doctor ordered to bring a smile of recognition to your face this holiday season.

On a deeper level, the Christmas and Kwanzaa holidays are also about creating meaningful ways to celebrate the love in our lives. Pearl Cleage's "Merry Xmas, Baby" and Nikki Giovanni's "Falalalalalalalala" both recall the struggle to take the psychological pressure off the holidays, to move from what "ought" to be happening to an appreciation of what is right in front of us. For all their wild and crazy antics, the Justices have figured out a way to incorporate Christmas and Kwanzaa into their lives and family celebrations. They, Sandra Kitt, and Imani Johnson-Burnett have all found personal solutions for incorporating the seven principles that may shine a light on your own holiday activities.

Our own Christmas/Kwanzaa celebrations have been inclusive affairs. The highlight of one season was our Imani brunch, to which in addition to the pot-luck dishes our friends contributed, they brought their personal stories of triumph over adversity, their poems, prayers, and affirmations for faith, hope, and forgiveness. Their love that day blended with the symbols of the season—the Christmas tree decorated with black angels and golden ribbon, a kinara fashioned from our collection of new and heirloom candle-holders, some of the recipes from chefs in this book—in one of the most beautiful holiday celebrations we've ever had.

Whether your own memories of Christmas and Kwanzaa are of the good times or the challenges, of being close to home or in a foreign land, it is important to remember there is a greater significance to our revelry. One of the deeper meanings can be found in the words we utter but only dimly understand—*peace on earth, goodwill toward all.* For as Rev. Martin Luther King, Jr. said in "A Christmas Sermon on Peace": "If we don't have goodwill toward men in this world, we will destroy ourselves by the misuse of our own instruments and our own power." Wise words to be used in our own lives and to guide our leaders and nation as well.

If the holidays are no more than occasions for parties, gifts, and food, then we have missed out on the true reason for the season, which Howard Thurman so eloquently expressed: ". . . to find the lost /to heal the broken/to feed the hungry/to release the prisoner / to rebuild the nations/to bring peace among brothers/to make music in the heart." It is the joy of moving beyond the material to experience the real meaning of Christmas and Kwanzaa that we wish for you and yours this and every year.

With best wishes for peace and the best of life's abundance,

Paula L. Woods and Felix H. Liddell

Los Angeles, California

ALLAN ROHAN CRITE, **THE MAGI**, 1937. LINOLEUM BLOCK PRINT,
COURTESY THE ALLAN ROHAN CRITE HOUSE MUSEUM, BOSTON, MA.

The evergreen singing aloud its poem of constant renewal,

The festive mood spreading lilting magic everywhere,

The gifts of recollection calling to heart the graces of life,

The star in the sky calling to mind the wisdom of hope,

This Is Christmas
by Howard Thurman

The warmth of candlelight glowing against the darkness,

The birth of a child linking past to future,

The symbol of love absorbing all violence.

This Is Christmas.

HORACE PIPPIN, **SUPPER TIME**, C. 1940. OIL ON BURNT-WOOD PANEL, 11 15/16 X 15 IN.
THE BARNES FOUNDATION, MERION STATION, PA.

✪ Christmas was approaching. Grandmother brought me materials, and I busied myself making some new garments and little playthings for my children. Were it not that hiring day is near at hand, and many families are fearfully looking forward to the probability of separation in a few days, Christmas might be a happy season for the poor slaves. Even slave mothers try to gladden the hearts of their little ones on that occasion. Benny and Ellen had their Christmas stocking filled. Their imprisoned mother could not have the privilege of witnessing their surprise and joy. But I had the pleasure of peeping at them as they went into the street with their new suits on. I heard Benny ask a little playmate whether Santa Claus brought him anything. "Yes," replied the boy; "but Santa Claus ain't a real man. It's the children's mothers that put things into the stockings." "No, that can't be," replied Benny, "for Santa Claus brought Ellen and me these new clothes, and my mother has been gone this long time."

How I longed to tell him that his mother made those garments, and that many a tear fell on them while she worked!

Every child rises early on Christmas morning to see the Johnkannaus. Without them, Christmas would be shorn of its greatest attraction. They consist of companies of slaves from the plantations, generally of the lower class. Two athletic men, in calico wrappers, have a net thrown over them, covered with all manner of bright-colored stripes. Cows' tails are fastened to their backs, and their heads are decorated with horns. A box, covered with sheepskin, is called the gumbo box. A dozen beat on this, while others strike triangles and jawbones, to which bands of dancers keep time. For a month previous they are composing songs, which are sung on this occasion. These companies, of a hundred each, turn out early in the morning, and are allowed to go round till twelve o'clock, begging for contributions. Not a door is left unvisited where there is the least chance of obtaining a penny or a glass of rum. They do not drink while they are out, but carry the rum home in jugs, to have a carousal. These Christmas donations frequently amount to twenty or thirty dollars. It is seldom that any white man or child refuses to give them a trifle. If he does, they regale his ears with the following song:

Poor massa, so dey say;
  Down in de heel, so dey say;
Got no money, so dey say;
  Not one shillin, so dey say;
God A'mighty bress you, so dey say.

Christmas is a day of feasting, with both white and colored people. Slaves who are lucky enough to have a few shillings are sure to spend them for good eating; and many a turkey and pig is captured, without saying, "By your leave, sir." Those who cannot obtain those cook a 'possum, or a raccoon, from which savory dishes can be made. My grandmother raised poultry and pigs for sale; and it was her established custom to have both a turkey and a pig roasted for Christmas dinner.

On this occasion, I was warned to keep extremely quiet, because two guests had been invited. One was the town constable, and the other was a free colored man, who tried to pass himself off for white, and who was always ready to do any mean work for the sake of currying favor with white people. My grandmother had a motive for inviting them. She managed to take them all over the house. All the rooms on the lower floor were thrown open for them to pass in and out; and after dinner, they were invited upstairs to look at a fine mockingbird my uncle had just brought home. There, too, the rooms were all thrown open, that they might look in. When I heard them talking on the piazza, my heart almost stood still. I knew this colored man had spent many nights hunting for me. Everybody knew he had the blood of a slave father in his veins; but for the sake of passing himself off for white, he was ready to kiss the slaveholders' feet. How I despised him! As for the constable, he wore no false colors. The duties of his office were despicable, but he was superior to his companion, inasmuch as he did not pretend to be what he was not. Any white man, who could raise money enough to buy a slave, would have considered himself degraded by being a constable; but the office enabled its possessor to exercise authority. If he found any slave out after nine o'clock, he could whip him as much as he liked; and that was a privilege to be coveted. When the guests were ready to depart, my grandmother gave each of them some of her nice pudding, as a present for their wives. Through my peep-hole I saw them go out of the gate, and I was glad when it closed after them. So passed the first Christmas in my den.

Tuskegee Institute

Tuskegee, Alabama

22 Dec 1903

My darling Mother—

It's now almost Christmas. I have already sent you Doctor Peabody's *Religion of an Educated Man* and Aunt Em two handkerchiefs, and am to send you as soon as it is finished a comfortable dressing gown. But, I feel very, very lonely here in these days so near Christmas—the day of all days when as boy or man I have, perhaps, most of all in the long year wished to be at my dear mother's knees. I can never forget the beautiful Christmases we used to have at home in Washington—just you and Papa and I. I was a youngster then but I'm sure I did not love you half as much as I love you now—and I loved you then with my whole heart. I can hardly realize that, perhaps, next Christmas our little family will mean you and Carrie and me and a little child. And from the bottom of my heart I long for that day.

Now, you are physically far away in Mississippi but you are spiritually as you are always, near to your boy. Your boy is a bit wayward and foolish, perhaps, but, Mama, he loves you and loves you devotedly. I want you to be happy. I want to make you happy. I sometimes think Papa, far away in some higher and better world, looks down upon me with a certain disappointment because I have not seen that you

ROBERT REID, **DURAS LANDSCAPE WITH SEA AT CAMERET SUR MER**, FRANCE, 1994.
WATERCOLOR ON ARCHES PAPER, 30 1/2 X 22 1/2 IN. COLLECTION OF MARION SKEIST,
COURTESY JUNE KELLY GALLERY, NEW YORK, NY.

released yourself from the petty worries and turmoil of the plantation and made your life, though serviceably active, serene. I think of this very often indeed but I don't know just what I can do. This is why I have rather hoped that you'd sell the old plantation—beautiful and full of promise though it be. There is here at Tuskegee the widest possible scope for your active service to a great cause and hence for your happiness—and mine.

Well, of the plantation—I can hear the cheery "Chris'mas gif'" from the little ones and the big ones crowding the steps Christmas morning. They are an humble folk—those poor colored people—but a sweet voiced, gentle folk. On the Bruce Plantation they receive, as they receive, perhaps, on no other, recognition of their essential worth as human beings and that is gratifying. In other words the plantation now means opportunity to these people and they would naturally have a keener sense of delight in Christmas Day.

I suppose most of us forget the spiritual significance with which Christian theology invests the day but there is certainly a deep beauty in the thought that here in the year 1903 there is set apart a day of rejoicing over the birth of a little child in Bethlehem. For this great bustling world of ours, with its infinite interest in the present and the immediate future, to celebrate the birth of that baby is really a beautiful thing.

Mr. [Booker T.] Washington reaches here on Thursday and so he will be with us on Christmas Day. The students and teachers will be glad to see the dear old man, who comes back for a short respite from his labors for us. I am sorry that he must forever be away from his dearest interests but I suppose he's been traveling so many years that to stop now would be death to him and his energy. So imperious is the command of habit! Well, he's a magnificent man and the longer I know [him,] the finer he seems to be. That, perhaps, is the highest compliment.

My bad cold is still bad but no worse; I hope it will leave me before long.

Carrie is as well as can be. Mrs. Ferguson looks well but is working pretty hard, I guess. Mrs. Washington is not well but looks so. Jane Clark looks haggard and worn. And everybody sends love to you—and among these are the students, who love you.

With oceans and oceans of love to my darling Mother, I am her

Devoted son

— Ros

Merry, merry Christmas to you and Aunt Em and Squire.

— Ros

CHRISTMAS *at* MELROSE
by Leslie Pinckney Hill

*C*ome home with me a little space
   And browse about our ancient place,
Lay by your wonted troubles here
   And have a turn of Christmas cheer.

These sober walls of weathered stone
   Can tell a romance of their own,
And these wide rooms of devious line
   Are kindly meant in their design.

Sometimes the north wind searches through,
   But he shall not be rude to you.
We'll light a log of generous girth
   For winter comfort, and the mirth

Of healthy children you shall see
   About a sparkling Christmas tree.
Eleanor, leader of the fold,
   Hermione with heart of gold,

Elaine with comprehending eyes,

 And two more yet of coddling size,

Natalie pondering all that's said,

 And Mary with the cherub head—

All these shall give you sweet content

 And care-destroying merriment,

While one with true madonna grace

 Moves round the glowing fireplace

Where father loves to muse aside

 And grandma sits in silent pride.

And you may chafe the wasting oak,

 Or freely pass the kindly joke

To mix with nuts and home-made cake

 And apples set on coals to bake.

Or some fine carol we will sing

 In honor of the Manger-King,

Or hear great Milton's organ verse

 Or Plato's dialogue rehearse

What Socrates with his last breath

 Sublimely said of life and death.

These dear delights we fain would share

 With friend and kinsman everywhere,

And from our door see them depart,

 Each with a little lighter heart.

What strange power does the sense of smell wield over the gates of memory? This morning, stepping into the cold, I sniffed a rush of snow-laden air that carried me back down the slope of yesterdays to a scene which I had completely forgotten. It was Christmas Eve in Philadelphia—a proper Christmas Eve, I remember, for outside the snow was falling softly, thickly, warmly, but within, the house was bright with Christmas spirit in every window. It was so like a conventional Christmas card, and I had so often wanted to experience the sensation of the weary traveller who struggles up the snow-laden road toward the glowing house, that yielding to the persuasions of a daring older sister, I ventured with her out into the street.

"Around the block" we ran, hatless and coatless, I believe, right in the face of the soft, warm, blurry snow. Oh, what a sense of adventure and what a feeling of joy and relief was ours when we got back to the sheltering house with its bright, dry rooms! We slipped in unnoticed except by another sister, who, perturbed by our vagrancy, had kept a discreet watch. She didn't tell on us—there's no fun in invoking punishment on Christmas Eve. Instead she produced unexpectedly a store of warm, soft ginger cookies fresh from the batch then in process of manufacture in the kitchen. Never ask me how she procured them.

Childhood, my own childhood certainly, photographs many such sharp detached pictures destined to return to one in later years with a wistful, indefinable poignancy. Sometimes does it not seem that the childish life was the real, the permanent thing, and that these grown-up days of flashing, restless achievement are hardly worth the long preparation which one in his teens and first twenties endures?

My first trip to France did not so completely, so lengthily absorb me as did the preparations which we children used to make for Christmas in that old square-roomed house in Philadelphia. I think we must have begun in November. There was always a tree and so every year "Christmas things" had to be made for it. Such a buying of such gorgeous materials! Glazed paper in marvelous colors, a soft, deep, yet bright blue; a warm, passionate red; a heart-of-the-melon pink. And because of the glaze on the paper all these colors possessed a curious, palpable quality; you could feel the color as well as see it. As a child I thought there must even be some way of absorbing it, especially that wonderful heartening, inspiring red. Besides the glazed paper there were sheets of thinner gold and silver with a slightly embossed figure; smaller sheets of gold stars, yards of tinsel, white, creamy paper lace, dozens of glass icicles and, of course, paper-dolls.

We made endless chains of the glowing colors and dressed the paper-dolls in tissue paper and lace. I had forgotten the possibilities of the tissue paper from which we contrived a round sort of pompoms, which were fancifully designated "snow-balls," and another round but differently shaped paper mass called "water-lilies." You made the snow-balls by twisting the ends of a circular piece of paper which had been slit down the edges into finger-width petals. Sometimes you gave too sharp a twist and the end of the petal came off. The water-lilies achieved their perfection with the aid of the head of the ordinary hat-pin. I cannot describe how this was done—the process is at once too simple and too intricate. Snow-balls and water-lilies alike were of all colors, but that discrepancy never troubled us.

Have I ever enjoyed anything since, I wonder, with the same intensity and the same sharp anticipation with which I enjoyed the Christmas season? There was a big square darkish room up in the top of the house where we children used to foregather and plan and plan for the holidays. Actually we had a little chant, *"Oh, won't it be joyous when Christmas comes! Oh, won't it be joyous when Christmas comes!"* You said it with a stress on the

WILLIAM MCKNIGHT FARROW, **RINGLING HOUSE**, N.D. ETCHING, 8 1/2 X 7 1/4 IN.
CLARK ATLANTA UNIVERSITY, COLLECTION OF AFRICAN AMERICAN ART, ATLANTA, GA.

second "won't," which converted it into a pleasing and irresistible rhythm which in itself created that joy you were so happily anticipating. I think that whatever modicum of unselfishness or generosity I now possess dates back from those days. For it was then I learned the sheer joy of giving. We children gave, I fear, with too little discrimination. Neckties and whisk-brooms for my father, and handkerchiefs for my mother. We could not think of anything else to give but we wanted to give. Gloves sometimes, perhaps, but that strained our tiny purses. It took two donors to provide one pair of gloves. My poor parents! They must have groaned at the inevitability of those unvarying presents.

Christmas Day when one is grown up is apt to be stodgy, too redolent of the taste of "the day after the night before." But the Christmas Day of my childhood was an endless round of new joys. First the stockings, always an orange in the toe and then quantities and quantities of nuts and raisins and candies. I can see us children now rushing from our rooms down the dark, chilly stairs, and exclaiming: "Oh, he did come, he did come! That's my stocking, see, I pinned my name on it." There was a bright, thin tinkle of happy, girlish voices and at intervals the discontented undertones of my brothers complaining because their stockings were not as long as ours. My mother always hung up my father's socks for them, I don't know why.

Some grown-ups complain because they were fooled by the Santa Claus myth, but I have always been glad of it. Surely there can be no lovelier way of starting one's own private little output of faith, hope and charity than this conception of an embodied spirit of kindness, riding red-faced and jolly throughout the land. I was a big girl, almost ready for high school, before I began seriously to consider the extreme inadequacy of any chimney-place of ours for a possible Santa Claus. Gradually I drifted into the truth of the matter, but I have never regretted for a moment the sweet foolery of my first belief.

But to return to the joy of Christmas Day. After the discovery of the bursting stockings, there were the presents to be examined. We received dolls—for which I did not care very much—useful presents—a dress, a coat, a cap; and books. And that was my reason for liking Christmas! After the long, wonderful dinner with its plethora of turkey and cranberry sauce, there was the long, dark, cozy afternoon to be spent in reading. There were always relatives at Christmas dinner, and these and the rest of the household, it is to be presumed, disported themselves according to their various tastes. My own idea of indoor sport was to lie on the floor midway between the gorgeous tree and the glowing fire and to bury my head, my mind, my whole being, in some fairy tale or strange romance. I had been taught to read when I was just past babyhood. Small wonder that at eight someone either with or without (I've never been able to determine which) a sense of humor gave me a copy of *Don Quixote,* the hardest nut which my childish mind ever tried to crack. I missed the broad farce and the sly wit which I am told penetrates that book. Doubtless I was a humorless child and took the story seriously. I know to this day I can never become interested in it.

What I did read with interest, with amazement, with resentment, with tears, was *Uncle Tom's Cabin.* It lay a grayish brown volume, thick-leaved and large-lettered, on the kidney-shaped table in our parlor. It belonged to my grandmother, whom I had never seen. But I had seen the book, and though the sight of most books was a challenge to me, I had never glanced inside this one. But on a certain Christmas Day, weary of Rose-Red and Snow-White, I happened to peep within those prim covers. They had to pry the book from my unwilling fingers. At the end of three or four days I had read it all, every word of it. I do not think I have ever opened it since, but the story remains part of my permanent mental furnishings.

Supper on Christmas Night was negligible. Probably there would not have been any had it not been for "the boys." But the time after supper stands out bright and sharp before me. Those relatives and older ones probably went on later to their own devices, but we children grouped ourselves together and sang hymns, beautiful, immortal, glorious hymns: "Holy Night"; "Joy to the World"; "Oh! Come All Ye Faithful" (my father's favorite); and "Hark! The Herald Angels Sing." How sweet and solemn and altogether lovely that time was. I have felt the rush of wings....

My mother's favorite song was one which had nothing to do with the Christmas tide but which embodied the spirit of life in the house. It began "When the woods are dim and dreary" and asked "What then?" The refrain was as I well remember:

> *Ah! In spite of wind and weather,*
> *'Round the fireside gleaming bright,*
> *We will sing old songs together,*
> *All the merry winter night!*

Can anything more exquisitely define home? Ah, lovely little pictures of the heart borne back to me across the years on a breath of snow-laden air! They re-create for me each season of the Nativity the spirit of a Merry Christmas.

Who gives himself with his gift, feeds three;
Himself, his hungry neighbor, and Me.

It was Christmas Eve by the calendar and the custom of men. But Christmas isn't Christmas when you're marooned in a boarding school in the far South in Louisiana. It's just one more day. Moreover, it simply could not be Christmas Eve. It was too hot; home was too far away; and as I crept into bed I half expected to hear a rising bell break in upon sweet dreams at the unholy hour of six-thirty the next morning. And then I began to remember that I couldn't even wait until six-thirty. I must rise with the dawn. Now, I have seen dawn in all its mysteries and promise breaking over shadowing mountains and limitless plains, over peaceful deep and turbulent streams; I have seen it creep upon the crowded skylines of the great cities of the world and gild the steeple of a village church. But to these dawns, dawn in the swamp lands of Louisiana is as Hades to Heaven—antithesis. For dawn in Louisiana is not a lovely thing, dew-pearled or even dew-drenched. It is sullen and soggy; gnarled and groggy. It comes grudgingly, relapsing now and again into dank shadows and leaving in its wake a long interval of gray chill before the arrival of the sun.

On Christmas morning, then, I was to fare forth in such a dawn, for the task of directing some students in the distribution of Christmas baskets to the poor of the neighboring countryside was mine. The anticipation of this evoked no particular pleasure and I fell asleep with visions of sugar cane stalks, muddy roads, draughty cabins and Christmas baskets chasing each other through my head.

Was I dreaming? No, I could hear it coming nearer, the sound of horns blending beautifully the strains of the century-old paean, louder and louder the music grew, and then just outside my window, passing into yet another Christmas carol, it began to grow more soft as the school brass quartette went on into the village a scant half mile away. With yet three quarters of an hour before I was needed to be ready to be on my way, I settled down for a short nap, and was on that drowsy borderland between sleep and consciousness when once more music broke the stillness of the early morning. This time, it was mixed voices, so soft that one just barely heard them, but soon they came nearer. "Hark, the herald angels sing!" I was wide awake and slowly I caught the spirit. It *was* Christmas morning.

There were two trucks loaded with baskets to be distributed far and wide that morning and I was a bit dismayed on leaving the school as I surveyed the itinerary in my hands. But my heart was light; I had forgotten the dawn; for was it not Christmas morning? A part of the chorus that had caroled earlier in the morning was with us as, leaving the trucks in the road, we turned up the pathway to leave our first basket and the fifty-cent piece which the Sunday School had sent. They began to chant "Christmas time is here, Noel we gladly sing." At the sound the door of the cabin flew open and a gaunt black woman in a drab and faded gingham dress, clasping a newborn babe to her breast, stared wonderingly. Then seeing that we came to her she cried, "Christmas gift," in a voice that trembled with excitement and emotion. She received our gifts regally but her thanks were broken and breathless. As she blessed the gift bearers, silent tears coursed down her cheeks.

One of our group, a girl just turned fifteen, begged to hold the infant for just one minute. The mother surrendered her child and, with trembling hands, broke a white rose from the one bush that grew near her door and, stripping it of thorns, placed it midst the holly that was on my coat. It was Christmas morning and the mother of a newborn babe had given me a rose.

EDWARD B. WEBSTER, **THE NATIVITY,** 1956. OIL ON CANVAS, 21 7/8 X 27 7/8 IN.
NATIONAL MUSEUM OF AMERICAN ART, SMITHSONIAN INSTITUTION, WASHINGTON, D.C.

A Christmas Carol

by Frances E.W. Harper

The Child is born, the Child is born,
So sang the angels on that morn;
When all the jasper streets above,
O'erflower with joy, peace and love.

Throughout the bright and vast domain,
In joyous tones outgushed the strain
And fragrance fainted on the air
From every golden vial there.

The burden of this heavenly strain
Was joy for grief, was ease for pain;
Instead of darkness, death and strife,
It sang of light, of love and life.

Oh, holy child, by thy dear love,
Draw our poor hearts to things above;
Unto our feet that go astray,
Oh, be the new and living way.

Oh, fill our souls with thy great peace,
A stream whose flow shall never cease;
To our dim eyes and longing sight,
Reveal the true and only light.

Now when Jesus was born in Benin of Nigeria in the days of English rule, behold, there came wise men from the East of London.

Saying, Where is he that is born King of the Blacks? For we have seen his star in the east, and are come to worship him.

When the Prime Minister had heard these things, he was troubled, and all England with him.

And when he had gathered all the chief priests and scholars of the land together, he demanded of them where this new Christ should be born.

And they said unto him, in Benin of Nigeria: for thus it was written by the prophet:

And thou Benin, in the land of Nigeria, art not the least among the princes of Africa: for out of thee shall come a Governor, that shall rule my Negro people.

Then the Prime Minister, when he had privily called the wise men, inquired of them diligently what time the star appeared.

And he sent them to Benin, and said, "Go and search diligently for the young child; and when ye have found him, bring me word again, that I may come and worship him also."

When they had heard the Premier, they departed; and lo, the star, which they saw in the east, went before them, till it came and stood over where the young child was.

When they saw the star, they rejoiced with exceeding great joy.

And when they were come into the house, they saw the young child with Mary his mother, and fell down, and worshipped him: and when they had opened their treasures, they presented unto him gifts: gold and medicine and perfume.

ELIJAH PIERCE, **BOOK OF WOOD, RELIGIOUS RELIEF SERIES, 36. PANEL 1, RECTO**, CA. 1932.
CARVED AND PAINTED WOOD RELIEFS WITH GLITTER, MOUNTED TO PAINTED COMMERCIAL
WOOD PANELING, 27 1/8 X 30 3/4 IN. COLUMBUS MUSEUM OF ART, OHIO: MUSEUM PURCHASE.

And being warned of God in a dream that they should not return to England, they departed in to their own country another way.

Save one, and he was black. And his own country was the country where he was; so the black Wise Man lingered by the cradle and the newborn babe.

The perfume of his gift rose and filled the house until through it and afar came the dim form of years and multitudes. And the child, seeing the multitudes, opened his mouth and taught them, saying:

BLESSED ARE POOR FOLKS for they shall go to heaven.

BLESSED ARE SAD FOLKS for someone will bring them joy.

BLESSED ARE THEY THAT SUBMIT TO HURTS for they shall sometime own the world.

BLESSED ARE THEY THAT WANT TO DO RIGHT for they shall get their wish.

BLESSED ARE THOSE WHO DO NOT SEEK REVENGE for vengeance will not seek them.

BLESSED ARE THE PURE for they shall see God.

BLESSED ARE THOSE WHO WILL NOT FIGHT for they are God's children.

BLESSED ARE THOSE WHOM PEOPLE LIKE TO INJURE for they shall sometime be happy.

BLESSED ARE YOU, BLACK FOLK, when men make fun of you and mob you and lie about you.

NEVER MIND AND BE GLAD FOR YOUR DAY WILL SURELY COME.

ALWAYS THE WORLD HAD RIDICULED ITS BETTER SOULS.

SELF-PORTRAIT 'ROUND MIDNIGHT

by Arnold J. Kemp

A man asleep on the bus, exhausted
by shopping the day before Christmas Eve,
bearded, on the breast of his wife or friend
in her fur collar becomes a handsome
boy again, his front teeth just growing in.

Waking early on winter mornings in
a humming house, while my family slept,
bathing, scrubbing until my skin wrinkled
and shocked when I stood out of hot water
to dry everything but my hair in soft

towels, I'd go back to bed and lie
there, naked, warm, and dreaming through
ugly beauty, the architecture of an old
house, a wet dog smell of a thousand white
hairs swelling underfoot like the wool of

clipped sheep, a body spread for the first time
like an iris pressed between white pages,
Da Vinci's "Proportions of the Human
Figure," prepared to make angels in the
falling snow, with a cold pain in the back

Of the knees and tears. Tonight the moon
is a light in the hands of a playful
child, flashing between rushing clouds
in a sky that talks with light. The woman
is shaking the man who wakes, laughing,

and I'm thinking that going home this time
can't bring home back to me.

PALMER C. HAYDEN, **RACCOON UP A PERSIMMON TREE,** N.D. OIL ON CANVAS, 33 X 24 IN.
COURTESY MUSEUM OF AFRICAN AMERICAN ART, LOS ANGELES, CA.

The meals that have the most memory for me are those that I shared with my family. There were eleven of us, nine girls with two boys at the very end, and I was the oldest. We lived out in the country in Madisonville, Louisiana. We didn't live on a farm, but we still grew our own fresh vegetables in little plots of gardens around the house. We had a big kitchen with a wood-burning stove and one room we called the dining room where we used to study by lamplight. Its only furnishings were a great big table and chairs made by my father and his brother. Sunday dinners were something, but I'll never forget Christmas; the holiday meal at Christmas is my very special food memory.

There was a special smell at Christmastime because we waited till Christmas to go with Daddy into the woods to get our Christmas tree. When we got it home, we tied oranges and apples to the tree.

The big cooking started on Christmas Eve. We went to Midnight Mass and then had Reveillon when we went home. In New Orleans today, Reveillon is like a festive dinner. Then, it was going home alone after Mass to something my mother could prepare in advance and leave with a cake for dessert. It was very plain, very simple, and painstakingly done. We'd have stewed chicken and a glass of wine and go to bed so that we could get up early and visit from house to house.

We had Christmas dinner in the middle of the day at about one o'clock, then put things out and picked at food all day. Contrary to what people in New Orleans have, our meal would be roast pork. My mother would do the best leg of pork. My parents raised hogs and the best pork was always saved for the holiday, when we'd have

ROAST LEG OF PORK

5-POUND PORK ROAST, BONE-IN

6 GARLIC CLOVES, PEELED

1 CUP ONIONS, CHOPPED

1 CUP CELERY, CHOPPED

3 MEDIUM SWEET POTATOES,
PEELED AND QUARTERED

2 TABLESPOONS SALT

1 TABLESPOON LAWRY'S
SEASONED SALT

3 TABLESPOONS BLACK PEPPER

1 CUP WATER

Preheat oven to 350 degrees.

Trim excess fat from pork. With point of knife, make six one-inch slits throughout the roast. Mix seasoned salt and black pepper. Fill each slit with salt and pepper mixture and insert a clove of garlic. Rub the remaining salt and pepper over the entire roast. Place in a roasting pan and sprinkle onion and celery over roast. Pour in water, cover pan with foil, and place in preheated oven. Cook for approximately two hours.

Remove foil and baste roast. Place sweet potatoes around roast and continue to cook about one hour more or until roast is done and sweet potatoes are tender.

— MAKES EIGHT GENEROUS SERVINGS —

pork roast with all of the little vegetables that went with it. We also had to have a beautiful boiled redfish, that was a special thing, and beans and gumbo and chicken. We seemed to cook everything we had.

People in the country did a lot of hunting and for Christmas we might also have a venison roast or ducks if we had them, roasted, or with a plum glaze over them. We'd have macaroni and cheese, and there was never any meal without potato salad. We usually didn't have big red apples other than at Christmastime and Mother would put one of them into the potato salad along with string beans that had been slightly steamed and celery and eggs.

At Christmas we also took great pains with the table. We had things we didn't have ordinarily. We used a starch-stiffened tablecloth. We had celery stalks with the strings all taken out in a glass on the table and olives. We didn't know they were relish trays. My mother hated to wash dishes, so during weekdays when not doing festive things, we had to eat the meal and dessert on the same plate. On festive days, we had an extra saucer for dessert.

Most of all, I remember the desserts we had. At Christmas in the country, you made cakes. Not just one, but many, all baked in our wood stove. People would come to visit and you served cakes—thin layers of yellow cake spread with strawberry jam made from our strawberries and then topped with a butter or sugar icing. We had sweet potato pie and pumpkin pie and the candies, fudge, and pulling candy like taffy with molasses that we had all helped to make. The cooking together is what made the meal special. I will never forget those festive meals we took great pains in preparing.

WILLIAM H. JOHNSON, **YOUNG PASTRY COOK**, CA. 1928–1930. OIL ON CANVAS, 31 3/4 X 22 5/8 IN.
NATIONAL MUSEUM OF AMERICAN ART, SMITHSONIAN INSTITUTION, WASHINGTON, D.C.
GIFT OF THE HARMON FOUNDATION.

When I was growing up in Brooklyn our family's Christmas meals were never elaborate for two reasons: one, my mother really didn't have exotic tastes and two, the number of dishes we had depended on whether my father had to work on Christmas. He was a chef for Restaurant Associates in the days when they owned all the major restaurants like The Four Seasons and La Fonda del Sol in New York City, so he wasn't home a lot. But he generally made an exception for Christmas Day.

I remember our Christmas breakfasts were simple; my sister and I playing in the living room with all the presents and my father in the kitchen making biscuits and slab bacon. For dinner he made things like oyster or chestnut stuffing to go with the turkey, and a couple of Christmases he even cooked a whole suckling pig. My uncle would be there and sometimes my father's mother. She was quite old when I was little, and she didn't get too involved in the Christmas cooking.

But when we'd go down South, to Florida, that's when I'd get some of that good "grandmother cooking" from my mother's mother. I remember Grandma Eva getting up way before sunrise, four or five o'clock in the morning, to go catfishing. She'd come back later in the morning, and while we kids would be in the backyard, playing, she would cut greens to go with the catfish. She'd even grind her own cornmeal to make cornbread. Grandma Eva did so much cooking for us, and was so good at it, there was hardly anything special any of us could cook for her. The one exception was my father's beer-batter shrimp. She loved that more than anything, so whenever we went to Florida for the holidays, my father would make a big batch of

CLAY POT ROASTED PHEASANT WITH MADEIRA, SWEET POTATOES, AND APPLES

3 LARGE SWEET POTATOES
(YAM VARIETY)

2 FEMALE PHEASANTS,
CLEANED AND TRUSSED FOR ROASTING

SALT, PEPPER

3 SHALLOTS, SLICED

1 CARROT, SLICED

1 CLOVE GARLIC, CRUSHED

1/2 CUP MADEIRA

4 GRANNY SMITH APPLES,
PEELED AND CORED

FRESH THYME

LEMON JUICE

1 TABLESPOON DIET MARGARINE

FRESH SPRIGS OF THYME
AND CHERVIL FOR GARNISH

Place sweet potatoes on baking sheet and bake at 400°F until 3/4 done, about 30 minutes. Let cool, then peel and set aside. Soak clay pot according to manufacturer's instructions, about 15 minutes.

Season pheasants to taste with salt and pepper inside and out. Place shallots, carrot, and garlic in bottom of clay pot. Place birds on top and pour Madeira over. Add 1 sprig of thyme and cover. Place in cold oven, then turn oven to 400°F and bake 60 minutes.

Using small melon baller, remove as many perfect apple and potato balls as possible. Sprinkle apples with a small amount of lemon juice to prevent browning. Set aside.

Remove birds from pot and let stand about 10 minutes. Cover with foil and keep warm.

Melt margarine in nonstick skillet and sauté apple balls until just tender. Add sweet potatoes and heat through.

Untruss birds and carve into halves. Place on platter surrounded by potatoes and apples. Pour sauce left in clay pot over birds. Garnish with chervil and additional sprigs of thyme, if desired.

— MAKES FOUR SERVINGS —

golden beer-batter shrimp just for her. And when I got older and visited Grandma Eva on my own, I'd make it for her, too.

My fondest Christmas memories are centered around the kitchen, especially as I got older and my father let me lend a little bit more of a hand during the holidays. First it was learning to make beer-batter shrimp and later it was baking biscuits. I would even sneak in the kitchen on Christmas morning and scramble eggs for breakfast. My sister wasn't interested in the cooking; she just ate and that was it. Even now, when she has my mother over for holiday dinner, it's not as big a deal as I like to make of Christmas dinners at my house.

Christmas for me is a time to gather the family together around good food and good feelings. My wife's mom is always there and at times we've had as many as twenty-five people for Christmas dinner. For me it's an opportunity to cook everything—roast duck, turkey, ham and roast beef. I always cook tons of food, but when I try to sneak in something exotic, someone objects because they're very traditional, not unlike my mother. I say, "Can't we do pheasant this year?" and my wife, Lynette, says, "No, I want turkey and ham—you know, like you always do."

That's hard for me to do, because I'm always experimenting. But I think I've found a formula that works for my family. One, we don't concentrate on low-fat cooking for the holidays. We may cook some low-fat dishes the rest of the year, but I have to sneak them in at Christmas. Two, I've found that holiday memories are associated with familiar tastes, so I don't fool around with them too much. For example, as much as I hate making sweet potato supreme with the marsh-mallows on top, it's a traditional

SMOKY CELERY ROOT SOUP

1 SLICE BACON, DICED

1 SMALL ONION, DICED

1 LEEK, WHITE PART ONLY, DICED

1/3 CUP LONG-GRAIN RICE

3 LARGE CELERY ROOTS, PEELED AND DICED

1 TO 1 1/2 QUARTS DEFATTED CHICKEN STOCK

BOUQUET GARNI

1/2 CUP MILK

SALT, PEPPER

SOUR CREAM, OPTIONAL

Sauté bacon until crisp. Remove bacon. Add onion and leek to fat in pan and cook until tender. Add rice, celery roots, 1 quart chicken stock, bacon, and bouquet garni. Bring to a boil, then reduce heat and simmer, covered, until rice and celery roots are tender, about 20 to 25 minutes.

Puree mixture in blender and strain. Return to boil, then stir in milk and season to taste with salt and pepper. Stir in remaining stock, if thinner soup is desired. Serve hot with a dollop of sour cream.

—MAKES SIX TO EIGHT —
GENEROUS SERVINGS

Note: Regular chicken stock and sour cream will affect fat content of the dish.

dish that everyone likes, so I end up making it. But I can't help it, I've got to sneak in something different. So maybe this year I'll make a sweet potato gratin, not with pineapple but with apples mixed in with the sweet potatoes.

COUSCOUS WITH PUMPKIN AND PINE NUTS

1 1/2 CUPS PEELED PUMPKIN OR SQUASH,
CUT INTO 1/2-INCH DICE

1 MEDIUM ONION, DICED

1 TABLESPOON OLIVE OIL

2 CUPS DEFATTED CHICKEN STOCK

LEAVES OF 1 SPRIG FRESH THYME

DASH GROUND CINNAMON

1 (10-OUNCE) PACKAGE OF
QUICK-COOKING COUSCOUS

SALT, PEPPER

1/2 CUP PINE NUTS, TOASTED

Steam or boil pumpkin until tender-crisp. Set aside.

Sauté onion in olive oil in nonstick pan over low heat
until just tender. Add to stock in saucepan. Bring
onion and stock to a boil. Add thyme, cinnamon,
and couscous. Stir, cover, and remove from heat. Let
stand 5 to 7 minutes or until liquid is absorbed.

Fluff with fork and season to taste with salt and
pepper. Stir in pumpkin and pine nuts.
Serve immediately.

— MAKES EIGHT CUPS —

*Note: Regular chicken stock will
affect fat content of the dish.*

If I could make the Christmas dinner of my dreams for my family, I'd try to blend the familiar with the creative, just enough of the traditional to remind us it's Christmas, but with some surprises to make the dinner memorable. First of all, I'd make dinner fairly informal in terms of attire and save the fanciness for the food. We never have soup at our Christmas dinners, so I'd probably start with a really great pumpkin or celery root soup, in some combination of flavors they've never had before. I love root vegetables, so I'd make parsnips and turnips and some other varieties we don't usually have. With the vegetables I'd make game—maybe pheasant with Madeira, sweet potatoes, and apples, or capon with gratin of oysters. Maybe I could sneak in an alternative grain, like couscous with pumpkin and pine nuts. The recipes I've used for celery root soup, pheasant, and the couscous all have a minimum of added fat, but as long as they don't sacrifice flavor (a key to satisfying my family), I think I can get away with it. But I've got to surround them with traditional dishes, so it would be back to tradition for dessert— a great apple pie, something chocolate, or a pumpkin marble cheesecake.

But the reality is I'll probably be in the kitchen this Christmas cooking the food my family loves. A turkey stuffed with crouton dressing and lots of celery, onions, and sausage, and a finely glazed ham, will be the centerpieces of the table. Old-fashioned turkey gravy, with and without giblets. Brussels sprouts, sweet potato supreme, glazed pearl onions for my mother-in-law, green beans, maybe some twice-baked potatoes. And if I'm lucky, I'll get to sneak in something a little different—I'm thinking about Jamaica peas and rice, or maybe a triple lemon tart for dessert....

When I was a girl growing up in the small farming community of Freetown, Virginia, preparations for Christmas started in early September, when we children went out to gather black walnuts, hickory nuts, and hazelnuts. Hazelnuts grew along the edge of the woods on low bushes, but hickories and black walnuts grew on tall trees, and we waited until they fell to the ground before racing the squirrels to collect them. The black walnuts and hickory nuts had to be gathered early in the fall to give them time to dry out in the sun to help in removing the outer shell. If they were not dry, it was almost impossible to crack their firm inner shells. When they were ready, we'd wedge an upturned flatiron between our knees, put a dried nut on the hard surface, and take a hammer to the nut. Using a nut pick or sometimes a hairpin, we'd pry the nutmeats from the shell—rich, flavorful nutmeats that, even on those warm, bright days, filled us with happy anticipation because we knew they would be baked into delicious Christmas cakes and cookies.

Whenever she saw a break of a day or two from the September harvest, Mother would set about making the fruitcake. It was a family affair that my older sister and I cheerfully participated in. Outside it might be rainy and blowing, but in the snug kitchen the sweet smells of dried fruit, grated fresh nutmeg, and spices kept us warm and happy. Mother bought the dried fruit from the store, and the fragrant mix of citron, dried candied lemon and orange peel, and seedless raisins seemed to us wonderfully exotic. We took turns chopping quantities of sticky fruit, which we then put into a big bowl and marinated with wine and brandy. The batter for the cake was so heavy we spelled each other during stirring or laid an extra hand on the sturdy wooden spoon. Finally, the cake was

HENRY OSSAWA TANNER, **STILL LIFE WITH FRUIT**, N.D. OIL ON CANVAS, 19 X 25 IN.
SCHOMBURG CENTER FOR RESEARCH IN BLACK CULTURE, ART AND ARTIFACTS DIVISION,
THE NEW YORK PUBLIC LIBRARY, ASTOR, LENOX AND TILDEN FOUNDATIONS, NEW YORK, NY.
PHOTO: MANU SASSOONIAN

mixed, and Mother spooned the batter into two prepared pans, where it sat overnight to marinate and mellow. The next day, whether it was still raining or not, Mother baked the cakes. When they had cooled completely, she wrapped them, still encased in the brown paper that lined the pans, in cheesecloth and put them in a large crock or lard can to age during the months before Christmas. Since most everyone cooked with lard in those days, wide-mouthed ten-gallon lard cans were common in every household. One cake was set on the bottom of the can, and a partition made of several slats of wood was propped over it so that a second cake could fit in the can. Every few weeks or so, we lifted out the cakes and sprinkled them with a glassful of brandy, rum, or whiskey to keep them moist and flavorful. Come Christmas, we unwrapped the cakes, sliced one up to give away, and put the other on the sideboard to be enjoyed by family and guests during the coming week.

In early December, as Christmas approached, we began baking cookies, pies, and cakes and, to our delight, making candy. We never had candy at any other time of the year, and so the chocolate and caramel fudge and peanut brittle we made at Christmas-time were treasured treats. All the candy was really sweet—just the way we liked it! Cookies were not as important at Christmas when I was young as they seem to be now or may have been in other communities; the ones we made were simple sugar cookies with no special decorations. At other times of the year, Mother baked thick chewy buttermilk cookies with sugary tops.

I always associate oysters with Christmas. The country store stocked barrels of shucked oysters, and we children were sent up to the store to fill our buckets with them. Mother made oyster stew for Christmas Eve supper, fried oysters with cornmeal coating for Christmas breakfast, and escalloped oysters for Christmas dinner. The fruitcake, cookies, pies, and candies came out on Christmas Eve—but only for show; we couldn't indulge until the next day. After Christmas Eve supper, we decorated the tree with strings of popcorn we had made a few days earlier. Sometimes we colored the popcorn with colored confectioners' sugar to add brightness to the tree. We also garlanded it with shiny twisted gold cord and often set little white candles nestled in puffs of cotton on the tree. I think I liked these candles best of all, even though they were never lit for fear of fire. Another of my favorite decorations was the red paper bells Mother hung about the house. They folded up flat for storage, but when opened, the bells were big and bold. Ropes of running cedar were strung all over the house until not a corner was left bare.

Christmas morning was heralded by fireworks. My father got us up before dawn and we huddled together in the cold, dark morning while he set off noisy Roman candles and lit our sparklers, which, as we became more awake and excited, we swung around and around, swooping up and down, making lovely trails of light. These fireworks were big excitement in Freetown for us children, and if our older neighbors did not completely share the excitement, well, that was all right. They knew they were set off by my father, the youngest parent in the community, and they had come to expect them every Christmas morning.

Mother always hung new long stockings by the fireplace for us after we had gone to bed on Christmas Eve, and after the fireworks we hurried inside to open them. There was always an orange in the toe of the stocking. By Christmas morning the gentle heat of the banked fire had warmed the oranges up so that their aroma trickled up the stairs to our rooms—our first Christmas greeting. There were also Brazil nuts and hazelnuts and little celluloid dolls. We did not get any other presents the way children do now.

After Christmas breakfast, Mother began preparing Christmas dinner, which was served at noon, early enough to give the men plenty of time at the table before twilight and chores. We invited some old people my grandfather's age and a friend or two, but mostly it was only our family (eight or ten of us, depending on which of our cousins were staying with us) who gathered around the table. Hog killing was just over, and there was fresh pork such as spareribs, liver pudding, and whatever else we had not put down to

EDNA LEWIS'S CHRISTMAS FRUITCAKE

1 CUP EACH: DICED (ABOUT 1/2 INCH)
GLAZED CANDIED ORANGE PEEL,
GLAZED CANDIED LEMON PEEL

2 CUPS DICED (ABOUT 1/2 INCH) CITRON

1 CUP CURRANTS

2 CUPS SEEDLESS RAISINS, CHOPPED

1/2 CUP EACH: DRY RED WINE AND BRANDY

3 1/2 CUPS ALL-PURPOSE FLOUR

1 TEASPOON GROUND CINNAMON

2 TEASPOONS FRESHLY GRATED NUTMEG

1 TEASPOON GROUND ALLSPICE

1/2 TEASPOON GROUND CLOVES

1/2 TEASPOON GROUND MACE

1 TEASPOON BAKING POWDER

1/2 TEASPOON SALT

1 CUP PLUS 6 TABLESPOONS
(2 3/4 STICKS) BUTTER, ROOM TEMPERATURE

2 CUPS BROWN SUGAR, PACKED

5 EGGS, SEPARATED

1/2 CUP SORGHUM MOLASSES

Mix all fruit in a large bowl. Add wine and brandy. Stir gently and let marinate for a few hours.

Butter one 10-inch tube pan or two loaf pans. Line with parchment paper. Butter the paper. Sift flour with spices twice. Add baking powder and salt and sift again.

In a large bowl, cream butter until satiny. Add sugar and beat with electric mixer until light and fluffy. Add lightly beaten egg yolks. Mix well. Add the flour-spice mixture a little at a time, stirring well after each addition. When the flour is thoroughly incorporated, add the molasses and stir. Add fruit and any soaking liquid in the bowl.

Beat egg whites in a grease-free bowl with a clean beater until they hold stiff peaks. Fold into cake batter thoroughly. Spoon mixture into prepared pan(s). Cover loosely with a clean cloth and let rest overnight in a cool place to mellow.

On the next day, heat oven to 250 degrees. Place pan(s) on middle rack and bake for 3 1/2 to 4 hours. After the first 1 1/2 hours, cover pan with brown paper (do not use foil) or place in a paper bag and return to oven.

After baking 3 1/2 hours, remove cake from the oven and listen for any quiet, bubbling noises. If you "hear" the cake, it needs more baking. When a toothpick or cake tester comes out of the center of the cake clean, it is ready. Set aside to cool.

When completely cool, turn cake out of the pan(s), leaving on the paper lining. Wrap cake with parchment, then aluminum foil, and pack in a tin. Homemade fruitcakes need air, so punch a few holes in the lid or set the cover loosely on the tin.

Store in a cool, undisturbed place. Every two or three weeks until Christmas, open the foil and sprinkle the cake with a liqueur glassful of brandy, wine, or whiskey. The liquor will keep the cake moist and flavorful and help preserve it.

cure. In Freetown we grew, hunted, or foraged most of our food, so because it was hunting season, alongside the traditional escalloped oysters, the chicken, and the rabbit was a panful of quail or snipe. We had white and sweet potatoes, turnips, and a leafy green, which at that time of year usually was watercress. After the meal came dessert—mincemeat pie, caramel layer cake, coconut cake, fruitcake, and candy.

When we had finished eating, the visiting began. We ran out into the cold, darkening afternoon to our neighbors' houses, where we sampled some of their desserts or candies or whatever they offered. We had already exchanged some foods with the neighbors right after Christmas breakfast; now the back-and-forth visiting and eating would continue all week. The adults in Freetown worked hard the rest of the year, and they took full advantage of this week to relax and enjoy themselves. We also used this time to visit old friends who lived a distance from Freetown. It was bitter cold during December and January in Virginia, and after hitching the horse to the surrey, our parents bundled us children up under heavy blankets and off we went.

Christmas week always ended too soon for us. In a few days, though, it was New Year's Eve, when traditional black-eyed peas were made for good luck and we feasted on more meats and vegetables, as well as the leftover desserts from Christmas. We went to bed early as usual, but the adults stayed up and ate supper after midnight. On New Year's Day, Mother took down all the decorations, and when everything had been packed away in boxes for the next year, the house looked strangely bare. We were a little sad, but took comfort in the knowledge that the joyous week would repeat itself the next year and the one after that and after that. It had been a wonderful time of sharing and eating and visiting and good times.

How long has Christmas been gone? This is what I would always seem to be asking myself every year around late March or early April when I was a child. By that time, I had exhausted my energy and interest in all but a few of my toys. Those new duds my mother helped Santa Claus pick out for me seemed old now, just like last year's and the year before's Perry Como sweater, Buster Brown loafers, and shirts from the Carolina Cash stores. Mom always made sure Santa brought me lots of shirts because the collars on my shirts would slowly begin to change during the year, to fray and often disappear from view. You see, I ate them.

Not consciously or with deliberate intent. It happened gradually and almost without effort really. In class I would find myself for no apparent reason sucking on the well-starched tips of my collar, crunching down on the double-bonded, stitched seams, and being teased by Bonnie Saxon and Ronnie Pitts for having saliva-soaked ends by lunchtime. My mom tried putting salt, vinegar, and other weird potions on my collar tips in an effort to stop the devastation, but that only caused me to turn my attention to the top two buttons on the button-down collar.

Because of this ongoing problem and the damage I was doing to perfectly good shirts, by spring my mom (who was the premier dressmaker in all of Spartanburg, South Carolina) had no choice but to introduce a line of collarless shirtwear for me. I had new shirts and she had satisfaction. Santa would have been wise to have brought collarless shirts from the beginning, but it didn't matter, for as fate would have it, I eventually lost the taste for starched cotton.

I had so many conflicting emotions about Christmas that it was often quite confusing. Issues pressed upon me as the holiday grew near: What was Santa bringing me? What were others giving me? Did Grandpa get my wish list? Whose name would I pull in class? How many names were on my shopping list? Did I have enough money? And last, but most important, what was Mom making for dinner?

You see, I loved to eat. I had an enormous appetite, and food seemed to be the appropriate panacea for most things in life that fell short of expectations. Food could make even the best situations and emotions better, and when I was not dreaming about far-off places, action heroes, and Lionel trains, I dreamed of my favorite foods.

Christmas in all its goodness, colorful displays, and celebration fed my imagination and stretched the boundaries of the usual evening supper fare. I dreamed of brown-sugar-glazed candied yams with caramelized lemon slices, sweet cream peas with roasted pimentos and pearl onions, roast turkey, cornbread stuffing with spicy sage sausage or fresh oysters plucked from their shell the night before by me and Dad. I could eat more than my share, too—of yeast rolls rising high, triple-layered coconut cake, pumpkin custard pie, and the largest bowl of fresh fruit ambrosia you could imagine. All this caused me to count the days one by one with the anticipation of Christmas dinner!

I particularly remember the Christmas of 1961. I was nine years old and for the first time in my young life I was not asking Santa for a brand-new bike. In fact, a bike was the last toy I wanted, having had a nearly fatal accident the year before trying to outrun an automobile. With my friend Stanley holding on tight behind me, I drove us into Mr. John's old Buick at the intersection of Woodview and High. This only confirmed my worst fear, that the bike was slower than the car. Luckily Stanley wasn't hurt, but I plunged headfirst into that Buick's windshield, and after a mad rush to the hospital with Dad and a week of convalescence at Bull's Clinic, I returned, head wrapped and feelings still wounded. So 1961 found me contemplating robots, football gear, and a train set, and anticipating favorite relatives coming to town and the culinary delights that were a hallmark in our house on Christmas Day.

My mother would start preparing a week in advance. Every day there were cooking tasks to be performed. Usually for jobs like canning pears, making brandy-laced fruitcakes, bourbon-spiked plum puddings, or peanut brittle, I was Mom's helper, always ready to pick up a spoon and whip, stir, or mash. I was her prep chef, cutting dried and candied fruit, peeling pears, cracking the pecans and walnuts, chopping nut meats, and running short errands to Miss Hattie's store for some small but essential items forgotten at the larger market.

School was out for two weeks during the holidays, and Mom and Dad made sure my sisters and I were not idle for a moment while we were home. The house had to be readied, and that meant cleaning everything from floor to ceiling. During the day we cleaned or polished wood floors, walls, blinds, silver, copper pots, and Mom's fine china (used only on special occasions). Outside we washed windows and awnings. Mom would dry clean or make new living room drapes, Dad might reupholster his favorite chair, or together they would make new slipcovers for the sofa and wing-back chair. The best night of all was when Dad and I would bring home our Christmas tree. That year Dad and I went into the woods about five miles from our house and cut down what was probably a six-foot spruce tree with an ax he kept in the crawl space under the house. This fresh tree was placed in front of the large picture window in the living room and we spent much of the night after supper decorating and hanging ornaments all over it. Mom made wreaths for the door with bows and Dad hung outdoor lights in the trees in the front yard and around the picture window that framed our Christmas tree. The lights turned our house into a fairyland of merriment.

The day before Christmas Mom pulled in the troops (my sisters, Cynthia and Dolores, and me) for the last big push. The kitchen at this point rivaled Santa's workshop,

HORACE PIPPIN, **CHRISTMAS MORNING BREAKFAST,** (DETAIL) 1945. OIL ON FABRIC, 21 X 26 1/4 IN.
CINCINNATI ART MUSEUM, THE EDWIN AND VIRGINIA IRWIN MEMORIAL FUND, CINCINNATI, OH.

ALEXANDER SMALLS' PECAN PIE WITH SPICE CRUST

CRUST:

2 CUPS ALL-PURPOSE FLOUR, SIFTED
2 TABLESPOONS SUGAR
PINCH OF SALT
1/8 TEASPOON CINNAMON
1/8 TEASPOON NUTMEG
3/4 CUP SHORTENING
6 TABLESPOONS ICE WATER

FILLING:

1 1/2 CUPS PECANS HALVES
2 TABLESPOONS BUTTER, MELTED
1 CUP SUGAR
3 EGGS
1 CUP DARK KARO SYRUP
1 TEASPOON VANILLA EXTRACT
1 1/2 TEASPOONS ORANGE ZEST

Grease a 9-inch pie pan.

In a mixing bowl combine flour, sugar, salt, cinnamon, and nutmeg. Cut the shortening into the flour mixture until it resembles coarse meal. Gradually sprinkle in ice water while lightly kneading the dough by hand until it holds together. Gather into a ball, wrap in wax paper, and refrigerate one hour.

Preheat oven to 375 degrees.

Roll out the dough to 1/8-inch thickness. Line the prepared pan with the dough, trimming the extra dough away from the edges. Spread the pecans evenly on the bottom of the pan.

In a mixing bowl, combine the melted butter, 1 cup sugar, eggs, syrup, vanilla extract, and orange zest, gently whipping together until well-blended. Pour over the pecans.

Bake the pie at 375 degrees for 15 minutes, then lower the temperature to 350 degrees and cook for 35 minutes longer. Remove and let cool on a rack before cutting.

—MAKES SIX TO EIGHT SERVINGS—

with all of us working at top speed. Mom operated the stove, my older sister, Cynthia, mixed the cornbread, Dolores peeled the oranges and apples and grated coconut for ambrosia and cake frosting, and I rolled out dough for pecan pie.

There was no pie on earth like Johnnie Mae Smalls' pecan pie. She always added a special spice to the crust's usual ingredients of flour, salt, shortening, and ice water, usually a little nutmeg or cinnamon mixed with a bit of sugar. The filling, which by now I could mix with my eyes closed, was sweet and creamy. For each pie I broke three eggs into a large bowl and added about a cup of dark Karo corn syrup, the same amount of white sugar, a big spoonful of melted butter, and then I'd beat all that up. (By this time my apron, the table, and the seat I was kneeling on were a little sticky.) After placing the crust in the pie pans and doing the needed patch work on the tears in the dough (oh, I didn't forget to grease the pans), I then threw in these large pecans my sisters and I shelled earlier. Before pouring the liquid stuff over the pecans in the pie shell I added a teaspoon of vanilla extract and some zest from the orange peels discarded from the ambrosia. My masterpiece was placed in the oven for a little less than an hour, maybe 50 to 55 minutes. I couldn't wait for it to come out of the oven.

During the holidays we would listen to carols and songs by Sam Cooke, Nat "King" Cole, Mahalia Jackson, or Sarah Vaughan. We'd also sing Christmas songs or pop songs from the radio. I remember this as being some of our best times together.

The night before Christmas was the hardest night of the year for me. It was the night that the perfect stranger visited every child's house and left everything you wanted all year—toys! I could never sleep, partly because of the excitement of the gifts and the food, but mostly because this stranger was coming and would visit my room to see if I was sleeping. I was always first to arrive in the living room on Christmas morning. The tree was lit all night and under the blinking lights glistened all those wonderful gifts. We were not allowed to open presents without everyone on hand, so I first woke my sisters and then bounced up and down on my parents' bed until my point was made— it was time to get up!

All of the gifts lay under the tree while Mom made coffee and began to put food on the stove. My father (who always made breakfast on Christmas after watching us tear through wrapping paper and run toys all over the living room floor) began to prepare his smothered crab and baby shrimp dish to be served over hot grits, already boiling away compliments of Mom. As we played, the smells began to overcome us.

I didn't see it anywhere! My train—I had asked Santa for a train set. There were plenty of toys and clothes for me, cards and books, too, but no train in sight. Santa had in the past always brought me everything I wanted, so I was at a loss to explain the absence of my Lionel train set. Somehow I felt my parents sensed my pain as I struggled with my disappointment in silence. Then the doorbell rang. There in the doorway stood my best friend, with a great big box wrapped with bright gold paper and a bow. It was Grandpa and it didn't take long to figure out—he had my train!

Later Cynthia and Dolores set the table while Mom covered the smoked ham with the perfect pineapple rings, brown sugar, lemon juice, mustard, and allspice. By this time I had seven-minute fluff all over me as I pushed the frosting all over the tops and sides of what became a three-tiered yellow cake. Seeing Mom make the gravy was a sure sign that dinner was almost ready.

Bowls and platters crowding the table in no special order revealed the fruits of our labor. Mom and Dad's wedding china with the green band and gold trim framed the oval table, which was dressed in fine linen. Perfectly browned yeast rolls were pulled from the oven. My father appeared right on time to carve the turkey and grace the table. Dad was famous for his long, rambling, and very thankful graces. As a boy I had no problems saying prayers at night, but grace before eating was just cruel to a kid who wanted to eat as badly as I did.

I can't possibly tell you how long dinner went on. It seemed that a lifetime passed by while we indulged in what seemed to be the greatest pleasure of my life. How was it possible to experience anything more glorious or satisfying than Christmas dinner? After two helpings of everything and a sampling of cake, pie, and ambrosia, as full as I was, the only thing that got me out of my chair was the knowledge that as soon as I felt empty, I could start all over again, and again.

✳ Five below, and a recent blizzard had opened fresh napkins of snow on the corners of the windows. Despite the warmth of a hearth fire, a deep chill surrounded me, persistent like an aura. You could tell it was Christmas Eve in our house by the odd but agreeable fusion of smells: charred chestnuts, evergreen, and clove-scented baked apples. The kids were upstairs pretending to sleep, while I sat in the kitchen gathering ingredients for ginger biscuits. Ginger biscuits and Christmas were to me what okra is to gumbo: essential.

Not that they'd had a long history in the family; my Grummy invented ginger biscuits one Christmas Eve seven years ago, the year she began spending the winter holidays with us. Sweet chewy shortcakes, flecked with just the right amount of candied ginger, biscuits so flaky they layered like an accordion when you pulled them apart. Everyone liked them so much that she started making them, along with a jar of home-made lemon curd tucked in a linen-lined basket, crested with a lace doily tatted by her own graceful hands. She often worked late into the night. Ritually, I'd rise upon smelling the sweet ginger dough baking, and together we'd sit at the table eating biscuits daubed with sunshine-colored lemon curd, sipping hot spice tea by the light of a candle between us. *Simplicity is what good livin' is all about.*

Grummy lived with us for the last two of her ninety-four years. Not a wrinkle on her deep-brown face. Eccentric from day one. Small and meticulous. A giggler. A gossip. Broke her hip at the age of eighty-eight sledding a steep hill with the kids. Loved the ceremony of coming in from the cold. *It makes you seek out warmth.* I haven't sought out warmth since Grummy passed in the night without even saying goodbye. The grief still makes me numb.

At about ten o'clock Michael came in from the garage, a little cranky from assembling toys. I was a little excitable myself, as if I, too, were waiting for Santa. I made a pot of chamomile tea for us, which we drank by the fire before going to bed.

No matter how tightly Michael held on to me, no matter how much of the blanket I'd entomb myself with, I could not expel that tenacious chill! I arose and walked through the house in the opaque darkness, feeling my way around with my fingertips. It was four-thirty; quiet, as the dignity of early morning ought to be. In the kitchen I lit the oven to 400 degrees; after a pause it roared healthily. As I buttered a baking sheet, Beetle, our tomcat, began to fuss. From the pantry, I pulled out a large weathered bowl and placed it on the table. It had been passed on to Grummy: an ivory and blue porcelain antique mixing bowl with a gold diamond motif across the bottom half, a retirement gift from the woman whose house she cleaned for sixty years. Grummy didn't believe in anything *sittin' pretty.* She used this bowl as regularly as Tupperware. As I ran my fingers over the chipped edges, I tried to envision Grummy's proud sweet tears. She had taught herself to read and write, but refused to write down her recipes. *It'll never improve if you follow the same old rules.*

This would be my first time making the biscuits. Hesitating at first, I sifted together two cups of flour, two teaspoons of baking powder, half a teaspoon of salt, one-fourth cup of sugar, and two teaspoons of ground ginger into the bowl. The stairs creaked just then. Wind, I thought, or maybe the house is settling. I chopped up two tablespoons of crystallized ginger and put them aside while I worked half a stick of butter and one-fourth of a cup of shortening into the flour until it lay heaped in the bowl like coarse sand. Arthritis never slowed the speed of Grummy's fingers. Her hands moved like the wings of a hummingbird. *Slow fingers make tough, greasy biscuits.* I poured

GINGER BISCUITS

2 CUPS FLOUR, UNBLEACHED

2 TEASPOONS BAKING POWDER

1/2 TEASPOON SALT

1/4 CUP SUGAR

2 TEASPOONS GROUND GINGER

4 TABLESPOONS (1/2 STICK) UNSALTED
BUTTER, CHILLED

1/4 CUP SHORTENING, CHILLED

2 TABLESPOONS CRYSTALLIZED GINGER,
CHOPPED

1 TEASPOON BAKING SODA

2 TABLESPOONS HOT WATER

1 TABLESPOON MOLASSES

1/2 CUP BUTTERMILK

Preheat oven to 400 degrees.
Grease a large baking sheet and set aside.

Sift together flour, baking powder, salt, sugar, and
ginger into a large mixing bowl. Cut the butter and
shortening into the flour mixture until it resembles
coarse meal. Add the crystallized ginger.

Mix together baking soda, water, and molasses. Make
a well in the flour mixture and pour first the buttermilk and then the molasses mixture in the
center. With a fork, gently mix until a soft dough is
formed.

Turn dough out onto a floured board and knead ten
times. With a lightly floured rolling pin, roll dough
out to 1/2-inch thickness. With a 2-inch cutter,
stamp out eighteen biscuits and place an inch apart
on the baking sheet. Bake for 12 to 15 minutes, until
light golden brown on top.

—MAKES EIGHTEEN BISCUITS—

Serve warm with
Lemon Curd (recipe follows).

out one-half cup of buttermilk, and paused. What next?

The lingering chill prompted me to abandon my baking and head for a warmer spot in the house. I rekindled the fledgling fire and sought out a soft woolen throw to wrap around my shoulders. Huddled up in a chair by the fire, shivering, my arms stippled with goose bumps, I felt movement. I stared into the fire unblinking. Beetle slunk into my lap and began purring himself to sleep.

I was jolted awake by the wind kicking up fierce outside the window. Beetle, startled as well, rose on all fours, hunched, and pointed his tail to the ceiling. An icy-cool breeze brushed past my right ear. Without moving my head, I shifted my eyes to the right. Grummy was standing by the mantel, poised in her blue quilted full-length robe with coral trim. She was wearing that characteristic French braid that was twined around the perimeter of her small head. She wasn't smiling outright,

AARON DOUGLAS, **PORTRAIT OF A LADY,** N.D. THE AARON DOUGLAS COLLECTION,
THE AMISTAD RESEARCH CENTER–TULANE UNIVERSITY, NEW ORLEANS, LA.

but her eyes were twinkling. She didn't move. Neither did I.

"Grummy?"

No response.

She opened her mouth, slowly, as if her teeth were heavy, and in a whisper, said, *Mayonnaise.* She pronounced it *mine-aze.* The force of the word banished her from sight. I opened my eyes, not quite sure how long they'd been closed, or if, in fact, they had been.

Back in the kitchen, rummaging through the clutter in the refrigerator for what seemed like an eternity, looking for mayonnaise, I stopped suddenly and stood still for a long moment. Mayonnaise? *Common sense now, child.* Laughing, I remembered how she loved a good prank.

Grummy!

It was now clear that the fate of the ginger biscuits was in my hands. Thinking quickly, I mixed a teaspoon of baking soda with two tablespoons of

LEMON CURD

2 LEMONS

4 TABLESPOONS BUTTER (1/2 STICK)

3/4 CUP SUGAR

2 EGGS, WELL BEATEN

Grate peel from lemons and set aside. Juice the lemons and add to the grated peel. Melt butter over a double boiler and whisk in lemon mixture and sugar. When hot, slowly add beaten eggs and whisk until thickened. Pour into a heatproof jar and serve at room temperature.

hot water and a tablespoon of molas-ses. In the center of the flour mixture, I made a well and first poured in the buttermilk and then the molasses mixture. At the last minute, I remembered to add the chopped crystallized ginger. Giddily, I began kneading the dough, gently, the way Grummy did. *Count to ten and you're done.* I sprinkled flour on a cutting board, turned the dough out onto it, and briskly rolled it out to a thickness of one half of an inch. I punched out eighteen circles of dough with Grummy's cookie cutter and arranged them on the baking sheet. Twelve minutes later, my golden-brown biscuits were smelling to the high heavens.

Darkness began dissolving into the abiding pink of dawn, leaving a bruise-colored streak midway in the sky. I heard a familiar stirring upstairs. I felt refreshed even though I hadn't slept—although that was still in question. I opened a biscuit, liberating a burst of steam, and broke off a small piece. I slid it into my mouth and cautiously chewed. My own addition of molasses deepened the character and gave the biscuit a richer hue. Grummy would have approved. I felt a flood of emotion overtake me. As I swallowed the last of the biscuit, I felt a distant but familiar sensation return to me. I dropped my shawl from my shoulders—it was much too warm in here.

◈ Warm December morning light and shadow moved evenly on Chickamauga. There were a few small clouds. The hickory trees alongside the farmhouse facing highway 69 were majestic. They moved their limbs gently in the breeze.

At another time the four children, Gal, Grew, B.B., and Moses, had taken two heavy burlap bags full of pecans gathered from the ground around the hickory trees in to their grandfather, Grady Flower, and left them near where he sat, pale and bent and paralyzed, in his silver wheelchair.

Even earlier, before their grandmother, Thursday Flower, sent them to gather the smooth oval nuts, Grady had insisted on having them all brought into his room because, he said, he wanted to *see* 'em.

Nobody suspected what he really had in mind. Certainly he knew Thursday was planning to bake ten pecan pies. She'd talked about it enough, and the children walked around smacking their lips on the imaginary richness of the pies, saying *yum yum*.

At one point, while the boys were shaking the pecan trees, Thursday's black, bony face poked from a window. "You get outta that tree, Moses, 'fore you fall and break your neck! Let Grew and B.B. swing them limbs. You too little to be up there—stay on the ground and help your sister pick 'em up!"

Now Grady had had the pecans in his room, hoarding them for a long time. Wouldn't even let the kids sample one. And Thursday herself had tried to approach the burlap bags only once, days ago, but Grady turned her back with his hickory walking cane. Yet Thursday had not given up. She needed pecans for the pies and the pies

JOHN WESLEY HARDRICK, **WINTER LANDSCAPE**, 1945. OIL ON BOARD, 22 3/4 X 28 3/4 IN.
INDIANAPOLIS MUSEUM OF ART. GIFT OF THE INDIANAPOLIS CHAPTER OF LINKS.

were for Christmas presents. And Christmas was tomorrow.

Thursday knew Grady pretty well and figured he'd give in. It was just a matter of time. It was still early morning, and in time, sometime today, Grady would come around to seeing things her way.

Meanwhile, the boys were going to the woods shortly to get a tree. After that, Gal would help them cut paper decorations. Thursday had already shown them how. After supper, the children would crack pecans, and she could start the pies and the opossum and the rabbits, which her son, Slick John, would come later to kill. At that time he would also help the boys erect the tree in Grady's room. Bring a little warmth and cheer to the old man. No need to always have the tree in the front. Last year Grady never even saw the tree. Refused to leave his room the whole week from Christmas to New Year's Day. Not that that was so unusual: there were months and years when he saw nothing beyond his own bedroom in this huge house built by his own hands. Anyway, Thursday would bake some beans. Greens and peas, which she preferred, were scarce this time of year. She'd make plenty of cornbread loaded with crackling. She'd unpack the dry figs and place them in bowls tomorrow. There would be peanuts and oranges sent by her daughters.

Thursday left the kitchen window. She went up through the large, dark, cool house, up the back hallway, through the dining room, halfway up the front hallway, and turned into Grady's musty room. Grady was sitting before the blazing fire with a blue wool blanket over his legs. The orange light from the fireplace made his white hair seem pink. His head was hanging forward. Yes, he's asleep. Beyond him were the two bags of nuts. Grady's bed was directly behind him. Crossing in front of him and the fireplace was the only way to the burlap bags. Thursday stood there, a few inches from him, trying to weigh the moral quality of what she was tempted to do.

If she simply took the nuts she'd have to listen for days to his rage and hatred. But then she had to listen to his anger all the time anyway. He hated her plenty and she knew he would never forgive her, first, for having had a lover years ago and, second, for her good health. So why not take the pecans and make the pies and hope for the best? How would God judge her deed? Was the Devil telling her to do this? Though she was no longer a sinner, at times when she felt herself giving in to the Devil's prodding, she'd smile to herself. The Lord will forgive because it's not for myself and it is to make others happy.

She tipped past Grady. One in each hand, Thursday started dragging the bags out of their corner. They were too heavy to lift. Stepping backwards, something hard touched her rear. She stopped. Turned. Grady was holding out his walking cane to stop her. "What you think you doing, woman?"

"These are the pecans, ain't they? I'm going to bake some pies. I *told* you, Grady." She let the bags rest against each other.

"I planted them damn pecan trees over thirty years ago!" he yelled. "They're *mine!*" His eyes bulged. Spit hung from his toothless mouth.

"Yes, but my God, Grady, you can't *eat* 'em all!" From her long skinny hands she wiped pecan dust on her red-and-white checkerboard apron. She stood there looking at her broken husband and smelling the decay of his body. She tried to keep him clean but it wasn't an easy task. His white shirt had yellow stains every morning after coffee. Sometimes he'd wet his pants. Now, almost instinctively, while she spoke, she looked to see if he was dry. He was.

"*My* pecans," he mumbled. Sheepishly, he looked at the flames.

She sensed she was going to win him over now. "*Lord!* I don't know what to say! Grady, sometimes I think you done lost your mind. You act like you touched in the head. The way you carry on is a shame!" She stopped and reflected on what she'd said. The tone was the important element. It had been gentle and compassionate. She had to make him feel the proper amount of shame without making him angrier.

She waited a few minutes for him to respond but he said nothing. He continued to hang his head. She left the bags where they were, out of place—closer to his chair actually—and she walked away. At his doorway she turned and saw him poking, with his smooth walking cane, at the tops of the burlap bags, trying to cover the nuts. Soon now he'd have a change of heart.

In the kitchen she began washing the sweet potatoes and humming to herself. As the dirt fell away, their dark earth-red color emerged. In any mood, singing was natural. Thursday's lips began to move.

O, sinner man what you gonna do,

O, sinner man what you gonna do,

O, sinner man what you gonna do,

on Judgment Day?

The wooden bucket in which she worked was situated on a bench beneath one of the four kitchen windows. Beyond this window, at the edge of the yard, Thursday could see her youngest grandchild, little Gal, with pigtails and in a blue cotton dress, feeding the fat opossum through the hole in the top of the makeshift box in which he'd been kept now for seven weeks. The box was on short stilts. There were two other wooden boxes arranged the same way, with one side of each made of screen, and with a hole in the top. In each of these was a fat rabbit. The opossum was black and gray. The rabbits were brown and white. When Gal finished feeding the opossum, she patiently stuffed carrots and corn and bread crumbs, the same stuff she'd fed the prehensile-tailed creature, into the rabbit boxes. The wild animals had been caught by the boys in traps set in the woods. And, along with her usual duty of feeding the chickens, Thursday had assigned Gal to the task of fattening these restless animals for slaughter and ultimately for the delight of the holiday season. Watching the little girl, Thursday was aware that Gal had become attached to the animals, and this was bad.

Apparently Gal had already fed the chickens, because Thursday could hear the hens in the yard making a fuss over the feed. And the rooster grumbling. It was midday and this was the second feeding. Slick John would not come until five or six. By then maybe Grady would give up the pecans. Thursday now remembered she had earlier sent Moses to the cellar, a damp, dark, musty place beneath the house, to get more sweet potatoes. What was he doing down there? Loafing? And B.B. was taking an awful long time to feed the hogs. By now he should be bringing in the wood Grew was chopping out near the fig tree. She could hear the ax screeching in the wood each time it struck.

Soon the boys finished their chores and went off to the woods for the tree. Grew carried on his shoulder the long two-handled saw and B.B. and Moses carried the ropes. Though it was early afternoon the ground and undergrowth and bushes were still slightly damp from the night, because the sunlight this time of year was not very powerful. They went single file deep into the forest, searching for and reexamining trees they had already tentatively selected. It had to be the very best evergreen they could find. It should be straight and tall and noble. It would be a thing they'd erect in the house, and it had to have the finest qualities possible. They stopped, reconsidered, and rejected several before they found the right one—one they had not previously seen—at the edge of the canyon where the Indians used to commit suicide. When they saw it they each knew and there was no need to say anything.

But they had to be careful. This prince of an evergreen was right on the very edge, and if it were cut down the wrong way they'd lose it in the canyon. B.B. worked at one end of the saw and Grew at the other. Moses, pulling on a rope tied by lanky Grew midway up the sturdy tree, desperately tried to direct the way it would fall; and if he was successful, this meant he'd have to move pretty fast, since he was struggling with the rope right on the spot where the prize would fall.

The landing went well. Moses jumped to safety, and right away they started roping in the limbs to make it easier to carry.

Still, it was not easy getting it out of the woods. The path was narrow and dense and there was no road that led to their place.

When they arrived at the edge of the backyard, they saw their uncle Slick John wiping his hands on an old rag. His hands and clothes were bloody. Near him, spread out on the grass, were the slaughtered opossum and the two rabbits. Standing nearby next to the hedges was Gal, sobbing. She continued to cry with her thumb in her mouth and kept her eyes closed. The boys put down the tree to rest. They stood watching. A white hen was standing on the edge of the huge black kettle in which Thursday made lye soap. The rest of the chickens had gone away in fear of the killing and were now scurrying around the far side of the fig tree and the grapevine on stilts at the left side of the house.

Thursday stood on the back porch with a pan of water in her hands. She, too, was silently watching.

Slick, a little drunk as usual, smelling of cheap moonshine, finished cleaning his hands and went over to Gal. He squatted before her. She was his favorite. He took her in his big dirty arms. "Honey, don't you know people have to eat? It doesn't mean we don't like the animals. We just have to eat. They eat. You see them kill each other to eat. And besides, tomorrow is Christmas. Don't you want to have a happy Christmas dinner?"

She did not answer, but Slick John gently rocked her little body in his arms. A bubble of snot formed at the tip of her nose. And she laughed when it popped.

Hearing her laugh, Slick said, "Thatta girl!"

The boys picked up the tree and brought it up into the yard and let it down again at the steps. They did not want to watch Slick John pet Gal. He never showed them any sort of affection. Slick went over and looked at the tree. "Pretty fine tree. Y'all getting to be experts." He smiled. "I'll help you put it up."

After the tree stood erect in Grady's room, Thursday asked Slick John to try and talk to Grady about the pecans. He said he would try.

But it didn't work. Thursday waited in the hallway. Slick John came out. "He won't give 'em up, Ma. Just be patient with him. You know Pa."

Sure, she knew Pa all right.

The evergreen smelled good in the house. Slick John left to go home to his wife, Lucy. The children sat on the floor cutting out red, blue, green, yellow, silver, gold, purple, and orange paper strips, circles, triangles, stars, diamonds, loops, and bells to decorate the tree. Its odor mingled with the cooking smells coming from the kitchen. Though they'd had supper already, the aroma of the Christmas food pervading the house made them imagine they were hungry again. The pungent smells of baked sweet potatoes, beans, and wild meat swam in torrents throughout the house and beyond. As they used their blunt scissors, they chattered away about the glory of tomorrow.

They were on the floor near the tree. Grady was in front of the fireplace. The fire was weak, it needed wood. As the children talked among themselves, Thursday stood in the doorway behind them. They were unaware of her presence until she spoke. "Tomorrow is going to be a big heartbreak if your grandpa don't give us the pecans." She said it loud enough for the old man to hear.

They looked up at her face. But she was looking at her husband there across the room. She went over to his side and touched him.

"Grady." Her voice was low and smooth but firm. "The pecans was for the pies. It's not like I'm asking you for something for myself. You may hate me, but this is wrong. Lord knows you're wrong. I want to give our son and his wife two pies. And Mr. Hain Alcock. And Apostle Moskrey. I want to send some to our daughters too. And old folks who are alone out in Remus Road. Them people don't have nobody who care about them. They could just as well be dead. I figure the least I could do is give them a nice pecan pie on Christmas Day. I was going to take them over there myself."

Grady was pretending he hadn't heard. He looked at her quickly, then looked away nervously at the burlap bags. Then at the flames jumping in the fireplace.

"You know that set of books the judge gave you for Christmas when you was a little boy? Well, I was thinking about them today. They still in that closet over there, and I know they must have made you pretty happy. You kept them all these years. Took 'em with you to architecture school. They meant something to you. I know a pie ain't important as books, but a person living alone with nobody might really be thankful to get one. Just like you was about the books."

He looked again at Thursday. The children snickered.

"Thursday," he murmured, "what you waiting for? The pecans over here in the corner." He touched the bags with his cane, quickly and lightly, a magician about to make magic. "By the time you get to 'em they'll be rotted away."

Thursday suddenly kissed the side of his face. The first time in years. The old man hardly knew how to react. He blushed. He took a deep breath and spoke. "Now, would you give me my pipe—and take these dusty bags outta my way?"

Already the children were laughing. Gal clapped her hands together and shrieked. "Grandma kissed Grandpa!"

Thursday gave him his pipe and lit it for him and he smoked it with enjoyment. Grew and B.B. helped her drag the bags of nuts into the kitchen.

After Thursday helped Grady to bed, the children soon finished decorating the tree and went with her to the kitchen to crack nuts. The four of them, up past their bedtime, sat around the table using the nutcrackers—homemade gadgets. Some of the sweet oily kernels they popped into their mouths and ate. Meanwhile, Thursday worked skillfully with the eggs and butter, the vanilla and the pecans she kept taking from a pile on the table. While the children cracked nuts, she beat more eggs and mixed more butter. The huge black stove continued to roar. Once in a while Grew added a piece of wood to its fire. Thursday started humming and soon was singing.

Two big hosses hitched to a slide,
Me and my Jesus gonna take a ride.

And the children joined her, remembering the song from church. But as they sang, they kept their voices low so as not to wake Grady.

Before long Gal fell asleep, with her face on the table, and pretty soon Moses could not keep his eyes open either. He kept nodding. Grew and B.B. kept breaking the smooth-shelled nuts and occasionally eating the tasty kernels.

Finally, though, even Grew and B.B. gave in to sleepiness and Thursday said, "Y'all better go to bed." It was already past midnight.

Once the boys were asleep in their room and Gal in Thursday's bed, Thursday returned to the kitchen and finished baking the pies. The children had supplied enough pecans. She worked on with the patience of a miller until the rooster crowed and daylight turned at the edges of the windows, where the old green shades never fully covered them. Now, once the rooster started, he kept up his arrogant sound for over an hour.

Thursday finished the ten pies and the wild meat and the vegetables and placed them on the large table to cool. She dumped a little water on the fire in the pit of the stove. It made a sizzling sound and stopped suddenly. But the warmth stayed.

A Winter Twilight
by Angelina Weld Grimké

A silence slipping around like death,

    Yet chased by a whisper, a sigh, a breath;

One group of trees, lean, naked and cold,

    Inking their crests 'gainst a sky green-gold;

One path that knows where the corn flowers were;

    Lonely, apart, unyielding, one fir;

And over it softly leaning down,

    One star that I loved ere the fields went brown.

HUGHIE LEE-SMITH, **WINTER DAY**, 1949. OIL ON BOARD, 17 X 21 IN.
COURTESY OF THE JUNE KELLY GALLERY, NEW YORK, NY.

⭐ It was Christmas Eve. The tree, decorated earlier by the children, shone with tiny stars, and tinsel ran in rivers down its boughs. Janet sat in her kitchen sipping champagne, waiting for Michael to come home. She had been waiting since six that evening. Now it was twelve.

"Son of a bitch," she said to herself.

Aunt Reade, with eyes as sharp as an ancient bird's, had been there earlier and waited with Janet for as long as she could. "I don't know what's got into men these days," she said at ten. "When I was a girl and your Uncle Amos was alive, we used to do these things together. Christmas Day was filled with kinfolks—Aunt Lettie and all them was alive then—but Christmas Eve was always special between Amos and me." She had taken Janet's hands between her own and held them gently. "How's it been going between you two, honey? Are things going like they supposed to?"

At ten-thirty Janet served Aunt Reade the eggnog she had made when she came from work. They talked about the children, Michelle and David, until eleven, and then Aunt Reade went home. At midnight Janet went into the kitchen and opened the bottle of champagne she and Michael had been saving for Christmas Eve. "Let's drink this on an occasion like Christmas Eve or something," Michael had said when he placed the bottle on the kitchen table.

"Where did you get it?" Janet asked as she examined the bottle and placed it in the bottom of the refrigerator.

"It's a gift from Jim Allen," Michael explained with a broad smile on his face.

"The Overlook Gallery is giving me a show in July." He paused to get her reaction. "It's the 'first of many,' ol' man Overlook said. Jim bought it to congratulate me." He kissed her quickly on the chin. "Didn't I tell you my painting would pay off sooner or later?" Later that night they'd made love until three in the morning.

That was in May, and for eight months the champagne sat like a sentinel in the vegetable bin of the refrigerator—through the show, the fights, the loving, and through the summer, waiting for Christmas Eve.

As Janet sipped the champagne, its bubbles tickled her nose before they touched her lip, "I've turned to drink," she said wryly to herself. Aunt Reade's words about her cousin Ada came to her as she drained the glass of wine: "Child loved that man so much she turned to drinking. Girl aged so much in six months she looked like your Aunt Ruth. Ada never learned you got to take a man for being who he be, or else you pull up stakes and look in greener pastures."

"Here's to you, Cousin Ada," Janet said as she toasted the wall above the TV.

For the past two years, Michael had rented space in Jim Allen's loft. Each day after work, he went to paint and returned home at nine or ten. Recently he had been painting weekends as well, coming home only for dinner, and returning at two in the morning to crawl into bed beside Janet's sleeping form. It was as if he had another woman.

"Michael is a good man," Aunt Reade always said. The words "a good man" followed Michael's name whenever she spoke of him. Aunt Reade was right. Michael was a good man. Lately, however, an unspoken tension had hovered over Janet and him. When Janet thought about it, two names immediately came to mind: Jim Allen, because of who he was, and Veronica, because of who she might be.

Jim Allen had been Michael's instructor and mentor in art school and was now his best friend. Jim was in his forties, tall and good-looking, with five sons by three different women. He had believed in Michael's talent, encouraging him to paint when everyone else begged him to find a more practical way to spend his life. But Michael was an artist, Janet had known it from the moment he sketched her likeness on the back of a McDonald's hamburger sack. She loved that about him, but she loved the practical side as well.

They had met in data processing school, "my compromise with security," Michael called it on their first date. Yet a part of Michael soared beyond data processing, security, and even her and the children. Michael saw colors, moods, and shapes where Janet saw only one-dimensional lines. He could capture gaiety or terror with a few brief strokes of a ballpoint pen. Jim Allen knew that part of Michael more than she did, and it did bother her.

Michael's show at the Overlook in July featured a portrait of a woman entitled "Veronica" which he had done the year before. The eyes had struck Janet first. They were large and brown, flecked with gold, which contrasted with the deep molasses brown of the woman's face. The expression of gentle laughter captivated Janet and the half dozen other guests who surrounded the portrait and commented on Michael's talent.

The woman was looking at the portrait when Janet first noticed her. Hidden behind a sculpture, Janet watched her. She watched as her eyes searched for Michael, and when his eyes met hers, they exchanged a look, both lingering and tender, that haunted Janet for weeks after the show ended. Yet she never mentioned it to him. The sense of having glimpsed a part of him not meant for her discouraged Janet from confronting him. Michael and the woman had just looked at each other. Nothing had really changed between Janet and him. Yet Veronica and who and what she was to Michael picked at Janet's mind whenever he was late or tired or distant.

Her thoughts picked at it now as she sat in the kitchen. She remembered Michael's voice that morning, and now at it came back to her, teasing like a child's. *Let's celebrate tonight. I'll be home early. I've got some things I want to say to you.* He had kissed her, and his thick mustache had tickled the inside of her lip.

"I've got some things I want to say too!" Janet said as she thought about

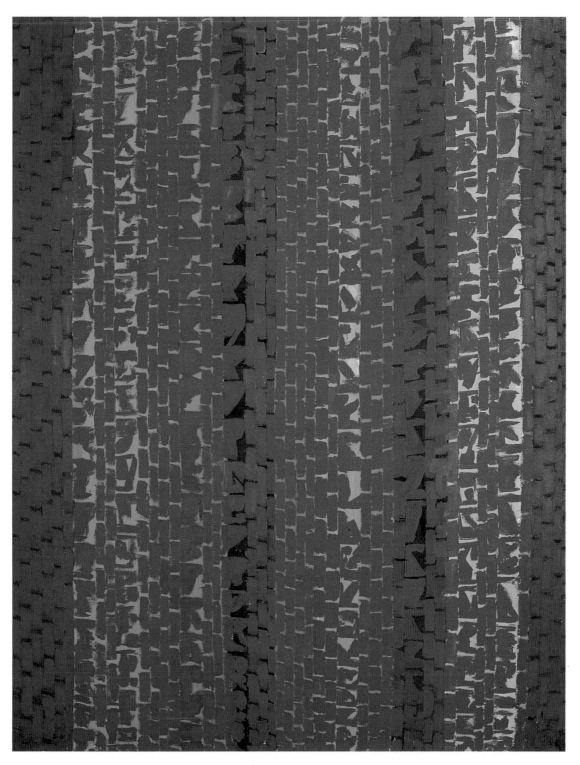

ALMA W. THOMAS, **RED SUNSET, OLD POND CONCERTO**, 1972. ACRYLIC ON CANVAS, 68 1/2 X 52 1/4 IN.
NATIONAL MUSEUM OF AMERICAN ART, SMITHSONIAN INSTITUTION, WASHINGTON, D.C.
GIFT OF THE WOODWARD FOUNDATION.

Veronica and her gold-flecked eyes. Her voice echoed in the tiny kitchen.

"Mommy!" David called suddenly from his room, jolting her from her thoughts.

Janet walked to the room where her children slept. Shadows from the hall light danced on David's face as she sat down on his bed. "Go back to sleep," she said gently. He closed his eyes and then snapped them open again.

"Were you talking to Santa Claus?"

"No, he's not here yet."

"Is Daddy here?"

Janet's mouth squeezed into a smirk, but she evened out her voice. "No, he's not here either." She touched him gently on the brow. "Go to sleep," she whispered and kissed him on the forehead.

In the pale hall light David's skin looked as soft as brown velvet, and for a moment Janet thought about his father. David looked like his father, but he was so much like Michael she often forgot it. He walked like Michael, talked like Michael and cut his hamburger like Michael. Only occasionally, in the twilight before she fell asleep or when she saw her son in this dim, faraway light, did she think about his father, and then she cut him from her mind quickly.

David's father promised marriage and "everlasting love" when she was two months pregnant but skipped to California two months after David was born. Her child was three years old before Janet trusted men enough to speak to them on the phone, and sometimes they didn't call back when she told them about David.

"You are better off without them," Aunt Reade said to comfort her. "He don't like the cow if he don't like the calf."

"But if I'd never had the calf ..." flashed though Janet's mind one April day when loneliness engulfed her like a fog. For weeks afterward, whenever David giggled or snuggled next to her at night, guilt slashed her like a knife.

Then Janet met Michael. There'd been a gentleness when he touched her or played with her son, and it penetrated that part of her that had grown as crusty and hard as an old scab.

"There's two kinds of men," Aunt Reade said when she met him. "There's that kind like that boy in there playing with your son, and there's them other kind, the ones too bitter to even hold you gentle when they lovin' you. Snatch that first kind quick as you snatch ripe berries and leave them others to rot, 'cause sure as hell, if you stay with them, they'll rot you right along beside them."

As Janet rose from David's bed, she glanced at Michelle, Michael and Janet's child, turning gently in the bed beside his. She stooped and kissed the braids woven across the top of her head.

On the way back to the kitchen Janet thought about the toys piled in the back of the hall closet. Coats and umbrellas blocked her way as she collected the toys, one by one, and carried them into the living room to place under the tree. When she pried open the cardboard box containing Michelle's doll carriage, the toy fell in a cascade of bolts, screws, and wheels into her lap. Cursing under her breath, she found a screwdriver, put the toy together, and kicked it into the lower branches of the tree. The carriage crashed with a soft thud that sent foam snow drifting silently to the floor. She slipped off her shoes and propped her feet on the crate they used as a coffee table. Renewed anger at Michael and his absence churned in her stomach, but it didn't keep her from falling asleep.

*   *   *   *

"Janet." Michael's voice called from far away. She rolled away from the sound, her face on the nubby buttons of the couch.

"What are you doing, sleeping here?" Michael nudged her as he sat down on the couch and pulled off his shoes. Janet opened one eye. Daylight streamed in through the living room windows.

"Michael," Janet's back hurt and her neck was sore. Her voice came out in a growl. "Michael, why didn't you come home last night?"

"I was over at Jim's." The mention of that name woke Janet immediately. She sat up and glared at him.

"Good morning," he said cheerfully. Janet looked away in irritation. The Christmas tree, still lit from the night before, glimmering in the daylight, mocked her with its cheer. David's new bike, leaning against the wall, caught her attention.

"At least you didn't forget David's bike," she snapped.

"I don't forget a lot of things," he said. "I don't forget how much I love you and—"

"Cut the bullshit," Janet said, narrowing her eyes.

"I don't forget how beautiful you are and how—"

"I don't forget how you make promises and break them before the end of the day." Janet interrupted belligerently, "and how we were going to 'sip our champagne' after Aunt Reade left last night. I won't forget that. Aunt Reade asked me last night how things were going between us. How are they going, Michael? You tell me. I sure don't know."

"They're going good for me," he said softly after a minute. His eyes, suddenly hurt, reminded her of David's and she looked quickly away. "They've been going good for me ever since we been together. I meant to get in last night, but I got involved working over at Jim's. Before I knew it, it was three. I thought I'd be better off just sacking out on the couch."

"Doesn't the great Jim Allen have a phone?" she asked, sarcasm underscoring her words. "When is it going to stop, Michael?"

"What?"

"Jim Allen, painting in his loft—" she hesitated. "Veronica." The name rolled off her lips and charged the air like lightning. Michael stiffened. His glance at the floor and then at Janet silently acknowledged everything.

"I haven't seen her in over a year," he finally said. The confirmation fell on her and Janet recoiled as if she'd been struck.

"Then you did!" Her voice was shrill.

Michael flinched. "It's been over a year since I've seen her."

"Michael!" His name scraped her throat.

"Janet, it didn't mean anything, not compared to you and the kids. You're what makes me happy. I haven't seen her since the show."

The show. The hurt Janet felt that day returned, and rage gripped her.

"You son of a bitch!" she screamed; but because she had thought the words so often that evening, they had lost their power. Michael did not react; instead he studied the walls, the tree, the ceiling, everything but Janet's eyes.

"You bastard!" Something violent inside Janet burst open when her mind flashed an image of Michael holding Veronica. She leaped at him, her eyes piercing with anger. Michael, quicker than she, grabbed her wrists, and they struggled.

"Get control of yourself and listen to me," Michael panted, his grasp tightening. Janet slowly relaxed and he released her. Dropping her hands to her sides, she turned her face away from him.

"I love you, Janet. More than I've ever loved anyone else. It was a passing thing. I don't think I meant that much to her either. It just happened once. I can't explain it. It's over."

"Why didn't you tell me when it was over?" Her voice was calmer now. She was out of breath, as if she'd been running.

"There was nothing to tell. I didn't want to hurt you."

"You've hurt me now," Janet said and glared at him.

"I'm sorry."

"That isn't good enough."

Michael held out his hands in supplication and, receiving no response, placed them on top of his head.

"What do you want me to do?"

"Give it up—all of it."

Michael looked at Janet in disbelief. "What do you mean?"

"You have to make a choice," Janet said smoothly. "Give up Jim Allen, his loft, the painting—all of it. It's that or me. I'm tired of sharing your time and now, it seems, your body with other people."

Michael sighed a long, sad, body-shaking sigh. After a few moments he spoke.

"I have to paint," he said gently yet defiantly. "I can't give it up, if that's the answer to your question."

A fire engine echoed in the distance, and laughter, loose and joyous, floated into the apartment from next door. Janet sat with her hands folded in her lap. Michael, his long fingers tapping the pillows on the couch, stared at the tree. Neither spoke. A glass bulb, carefully balanced on the tip of a limb by Michelle the night before, fell and splattered on the floor in filaments of red and silver.

"An omen," Michael said softly. Janet said nothing but stared straight ahead. Michael glanced at her from the corner of his eye and then stood up.

"Where do you think you're going?" Janet demanded.

Michael shrugged and answered curtly. "There's something I forgot."

Janet sat in the morning cool of the living room, wanting to cry. Tears had been there and gone in her rage. Now they came back. *You got to take a man for being who he be.* Aunt Reade's voice chimed in her mind.

"But how much do I take?" Janet asked aloud. She heard Michael dragging something through the front door, and she looked up.

"Here," he said, like a child surrendering a forbidden possession, as he propped a large and unframed canvas against the wall in front of her.

The painting was of her, done in shades of gold, brown, and red. Her figure sat stately and calm in a high-backed wooden chair, with one hand in her lap and the other on David, who sat on the floor beside her. Michelle, with cornrowed hair and thumb in mouth, leaned against her knee, clasping the hem of her skirt. They were surrounded by the sun, and its colors blended with their skin and burst forth in rays of gold and white from the outer edges of the canvas.

"Merry Christmas," Michael said, so softly she almost didn't hear him.

My Father's Telescope

by Rita Dove

The oldest joke

in the world,

a chair on three legs.

shrinks. After

years of cupboards

Sawdust kicks

and end tables, after

up, swirls

around his boots

a plywood Santa

and seven elves

and settles

for the lawn in snow,

in the cuffs of his

pants. The saw is

he knows.

He's failed, and

as nervous as

in oak.

a parrot.

The chair

Next Christmas

he buys himself

and his son

a telescope.

THE GIFT | *Dorothy West*

When I was ten years old I was accepted by the Girls' Latin School as a suitable candidate for admission to the sixth class, the level from which one progressed to the pinnacle of the first class. The average age of sixth-class students was twelve, which has a more impressive sound than ten. I was worried by that age gap which was compounded by the fact that I was small for my age and maybe looked as young as nine, an absurd situation for a student who, I had been told, was addressed by her teachers as "Miss."

I asked my mother if my classmates would make fun of me. In my lower school, attended by both boys and girls, the boys had made fun of me because I was colored. With them name-calling had been routine. In the Brahmin Boston of that day, boys of simple background needed a scapegoat for their self-esteem.

My mother's reassuring answer was that people of proper background never made fun of people because of conditions over which they had no control, like being ten, like being small for ten, like being colored. I must never forget, she reminded me, as she frequently reminded me, that I was my father's daughter. He had survived the condition of slavery. I would never face an endurance test more difficult than that.

So I went to the Latin School on opening day, holding my head erect, hearing myself formally addressed by my teachers, and not for a moment feeling that the title crowned my head unbecomingly. Then it was lunchtime and I made my way down the long hall to the lunchroom, never having even seen a school lunchroom before, or paid for a meal by myself before, but determined to treat it as an everyday occurrence, and not spill anything.

Two presumably first-class young women, tall and perfect in appearance, saw me, stopped dead in their tracks, enchanted by my difference, their faces spread with smiles. They rushed toward me, pulling me back and forth between them, one of them saying, she's my baby, the other one saying, no, she's mine.

In that comic tug and pull the title my teachers had conferred on me in my passage from childhood lost all meaning. I was stunned and speechless. Then I wriggled, found my voice, and said urgently, "Beg your pardon. I'm not a baby. I'm not really as little as I look. I'm ten years old."

At that, to my surprise, instead of sobering, they burst out laughing and walked away doubled over with mirth, the sound of which lingered with me for the rest of the day.

That encounter made me feel a great unease about another matter which I had never let surface, knowing my mother knew the truth of it but not yet sure I was ready to surrender my chosen belief to her reality. Nevertheless I wanted to avoid a misstep and stand on firm ground in front of the twelve-year-olds in my class. I could no longer put off facing the truth about Santa Claus.

If ten seems old not to know whether Santa Claus is real or not, that period in America's history was called the age of innocence for the general population, at least for those who had never had to struggle with want. I was one of those so blessed.

When my mother said that my father was Santa Claus, I wasn't demolished. I know I felt sad, but I think I felt relieved. Now I could talk to my classmates about Christmas without skirting around the edges. That I was shedding the last vestige of my childhood was not traumatic, considering that in return I saw my father in a special light.

Slavery ended when he was seven. His mother, who had been a cook, found hire in a boardinghouse, my father sharing her quarters, and shining shoes, running errands

WILLIAM MCKNIGHT FARROW, **CHRISTMAS EVE**, CA. 1927. ETCHING, COURTESY OF DU SABLE MUSEUM OF
AFRICAN AMERICAN HISTORY, GIFT OF MRS. IRVIN C. MOLLISON, CHICAGO, IL.
PHOTO: GARRY HENDERSON.

for the boarders, and putting his pennies and nickels and occasional dimes in a cigar box,
except for a small sum he paid an indigent townsman to teach him to read and write and
figure sums. The latter became one of my father's indispensable skills.

When he was eight or so, he went to the open market with the boardinghouse
owner to carry her baskets when they were laden, and watched her pick and choose, heard
her haggle over prices, listened to the market talk of the men. The Christmas that he was
ten he knew what he wanted. He wanted a business of his own. He got out his cigar box

with his savings, and asked his mother how much she had in savings. He told her, this ten-year-old man-boy, that he wanted to go into business for himself, he wanted a boarding-house of his own, If he could borrow her money and services, he promised that he would make her rich in return.

I am told that he did, that they had a boardinghouse and a restaurant in Richmond, Virginia, that my grandmother learned to wear silk.

My father moved on, as men seeking wider opportunities do. I don't think it ever occurred to him that his race and former condition of servitude might be handicaps. They were not. He came north to Springfield and apprenticed himself to a wholesale buyer of fruits and vegetables. When he learned the art of trading, he opened two stores, one a retail fruit store, the other an ice cream parlor, catering to those who could afford to eat fruit every day, to whom an ice cream parlor was a pleasant place to dally.

My father's dream was to be a wholesale merchant of fruits and vegetables in the venerable Boston Market. And so he was. His place of business was on South Market Street just opposite Faneuil Hall, and I will cherish forever the sound of the great dray horses' hooves on the cobblestones as I waited, with my hand in my mother's, to cross the street to my father's store, with its big banana rooms and the big store cat that thought small children were varmints to attack.

My father was a generation older than my mother. Yet I cannot imagine either one married to anyone else. I cannot imagine belonging to anybody else. On the Christmas of my father's tenth birthday he prepared my own coming of age in my tenth year on Christmas Day. Then I knew the gifts he had given me were endurance and strength of will. The tangible gifts were just extras.

My mother was not impressed with her beauty;

once a year she put it on like a costume,

plaited her black hair, slick as cornsilk, down past her hips

in one rope-thick braid, turned it, carefully, hand over hand,

and fixed it at the nape of her neck, stiff and elegant as a crown,

with tortoise pins, like huge insects,

     some belonging to her dead mother,

        some to my living grandmother.

Sitting on the stool at the mirror,

she applied a peachy foundation that seemed to hold her down, to trap her,

as if we never would have noticed what flew among us unless

  it was weighted and bound in its mask.

Vaseline shined her eyebrows,

mascara blackened her lashes until they swept down like feathers;

her eyes deepened until they shone from far away.

ALBERT V. CHONG, **AUNT WINNIE'S STORY**, 1994, ILFOCHROME PRINT, 30 X 20 IN.
COURTESY OF THE PHOTOGRAPHER.

Now I remember her hands, her poor hands, which, even then

were old from scrubbing,

whiter on the inside than they should have been,

and hard, the first joints of her fingers, little fattened pads,

the nails filed to sharp points like old-fashioned ink pens,

    painted a jolly color.

Her hands stood next to her face and wanted to be put away, prayed

for the scrub bucket and brush to make them useful.

And, as I write, I forget the years I watched her

pull hairs like a witch from her chin, magnify

every blotch—as if acid were thrown from the inside.

But once a year my mother

rose in her white silk slip,

not the slave of the house, the woman,

took the ironed dress from the hanger—

allowing me to stand on the bed, so that

my face looked directly into her face,

and hold the garment away from her

as she pulled it down.

MY MOTHER HATED BEING POOR (XMAS 1964) | *Pearl Cleage*

My mother hated being poor at Christmas. She hated being poor anytime, but Christmas just seemed to add insult to injury. It increased her irritation geometrically. Her parents had come through the Depression with barely a ripple in their household even when Mr. Ford laid my grandfather off. "I told Shell when we first got married," my grandmother told my mother—and whenever she told the story my mother told me— "I told Shell if you let me handle all the money, whenever you need some, you'll have some." And he did, and she did, and "We never were hungry," my mother would say.

And we weren't hungry this Christmas. We had a turkey. Which was the problem. My mother was cooking the turkey in the temporary stand-up oven we were using because our real oven had broken and we didn't have money enough to get it fixed. My Uncle Louis had had this stand-up thing in the garage for a long time and when my stepfather asked him if we could borrow it he said sure.

My mother hated borrowing anything from her in-laws, but she had to have something to cook the turkey in and this thing was the only possibility unless she just wasn't going to cook at all this Christmas, and that didn't seem to be an option, although I don't remember why we weren't going to one grandmother or another. But we weren't. We were eating at home as soon as the slower-than-it-should-be stand-up oven finished cooking the turkey, which my mother had expected out and on the table

84

almost an hour ago, but it wasn't quite done yet, and there is nothing worse than poultry with blood on the bone. So we were waiting.

The other food was ready and beginning to wilt just a little. There was a second skin on the gravy and the green beans were getting a little mushy. But mostly my mother was getting mad about being poor.

She was probably even madder, although I didn't understand this then, because she knew why we were poor and she couldn't argue it. She knew she had married into a family of people who spent their lives fighting white folks. Period. Not the most lucrative life's work in America.

The latest family venture was the publishing of a radical weekly tabloid, which was single-handedly raising the level of discussion in barbershops and poolrooms all over Detroit.

My mother shared the commitment and loved the paper, but it was, of course, making no money, and the press she and my stepfather had purchased to print it on was a huge West German monstrosity that was sucking money out the door as fast as it spit out the printed pink sheets of the paper. My mother was in the terrible position of loving the idea, and being an integral part of the struggle, but wishing the sacrifice wasn't always so present and so personal.

And the turkey was taking forever. Finally, she tested it one more time and it seemed to be ready. She lifted it out carefully and my sister and I breathed in the wonderful aroma of Christmas dinner. The turkey was perfectly brown. The homemade dressing was spilling out of one end, smelling of celery and sage, and the drumsticks were tucked demurely at the other. My mother smiled and relaxed for the first time that day, and then she saw the spot.

PALMER HAYDEN, **CHRISTMAS.** CA. 1939-40, OIL ON CANVAS, 27 X 34 1/2 IN.
COLLECTION OF BERNARD KING. COURTESY OF MICHAEL ROSENFELD GALLERY, NEW YORK, NY.

On the turkey's right breast, there was a blue spot about the size of a quarter. It was an ominous, metallic blue for a turkey breast. My mother touched it with her finger and frowned. She lifted the top of the freestanding oven, looked inside it, and there was a strange little twisted wire thing sticking out that had obviously lay on our turkey as it cooked and deposited some metallic junk on one of its beautiful breasts.

My sister and I looked at each other and then at my mother as she carefully, too carefully, laid the top down on the stove and called my stepfather. What she wanted to tell him was that the turkey was obviously metal poisoned by the strange wire; that we couldn't possibly eat it since we would all die instantly; that she was sorry but she was going to have to throw the whole thing away. What she wanted to imply was that it was his fault for not making enough money to fix her oven.

My stepfather, having walked into a hornet's nest completely unsuspecting, heard all this, looked from my mother's angry face to the almost perfect bird, and made a grave error. He laughed. My mother pursed her lips in the way that runs through generations of women in my family and stalked out of the room. My stepfather looked at my sister and me and grinned, but we were having none of it. We eased out of the room and left him alone with the bird.

My mother returned in a few minutes with a Kleenex clutched in her hand and her sunglasses on. This meant she had been upstairs crying and didn't want us to know it. I always wondered what could have been more obvious than sudden sunglasses at five in the afternoon inside the house, but it was none of my business.

We could hear them arguing quietly in the kitchen. My mother was determined to throw the tainted turkey out and my stepfather was trying to remain rational and save his Christmas dinner. The phone rang and my stepfather left the kitchen for a minute to answer it. By the time he got back, my mother was coming up the snow-covered back steps, brushing off her hands, and the turkey was lying in the garbage can behind our house.

"You're crazy," my stepfather said, amazed.

"I'm not going to kill my family just because we don't have money enough to fix a damn stove," said my mother. "That turkey wouldn't have killed anybody," said my stepfather in the deadly calm voice of someone determined not to argue but just as determined not to take a single step backward. "I ate a piece while you were out of the kitchen and I'm just fine."

And he was. He never even threw up, or got diarrhea, or botulism, or any of the other ills my mother had predicted. And I'm sure she was glad although she probably wouldn't have objected to a stomach cramp or two. We even ended up with a Christmas care package from my grandmother, delivered by my two grinning uncles, who had heard the story and came to try to help us save our Christmas, or what was left of it.

But my mother would not be comforted. She was still so mad she couldn't even appreciate the foil-covered plate of turkey and dressing my uncles unwrapped and offered with the perfect dose of don't-take-it-all-so-serious good humor. So they shrugged and smiled, backed away, and waited for my stepfather to redeem himself, although everybody knew he wasn't really a villain even if he had laughed when he should have shared her tears. My mother knew it too, but she did not seem to be in the mood for redemption, demanding as it does confession and forgiveness. Even though she understood everything, she didn't have to like it. Especially at Christmas.

GIFT
by Carol Freeman

christmas morning i

got up before the others and

ran

naked across the plank

floor into the front

room to see grandmama

sewing a new

button on my last year

ragdoll.

■■ she liked evaporated milk even though it cooled the coffee quicker than she could drink it. the thick milk made it sweet and the same color as she was, like kraft caramels when the cellophane is removed. she would sit at the breakfast table and stare at herself in the cup, take sips and suck her teeth

but not too many sips. she often left the table, too anxious, too angled into the list of things to be done that day to dawdle. so on saturdays and holidays there might be ten or fifteen cups of cold coffee sitting around with a deep impression of nefertiti red lipstick seductively stamped on the rim

even on this morning there was a cup nestled in its saucer on the radiator behind the xmas tree. one on the coffee table in front of the couch. one on the floor under the tree and one, her first of the day, on the dining room table. there were more in the kitchen

and in her hand was her favorite cup, bone white with blue irises trimmed in gold and a handle only her thin finger could fit. i watched it go to her mouth and she immediately set it down on the telephone table. in a moment she would head for the kitchen for a fresh one. it was xmas morning

i was standing on the stairs watching them. their argument had brought me from my room. the tinsel, candy cane wrappers, and shards of colored glass from broken ornaments were now huddled and homeless in the corner. the tree was an ornament he always waited until the night before to buy. it was cheaper then. it was always xmas by the time it was fully decorated. xmas was a ritual in which they gave us everything and we didn't know enough or have enough money to give them anything

WILLIAM MCKNIGHT FARROW, **THE MESSENGER**, N.D. ETCHING, 11 1/2 X 8 1/4 IN.
COURTESY CLARK ATLANTA UNIVERSITY, COLLECTION OF AFRICAN AMERICAN ART, ATLANTA, GA.

i'm convinced that this is where some of our shame had its beginning. who could ignore the shadow behind his torchlight smile? on that morning

the pressures of giving weighed like bags of creamy tan sand around his neck

and she took pleasure in the giving too but knew how heavy it was, how it would bend the bones in his back, maybe break it

so she told him not to do it. not to drive to hfc and politely beg the downtown white man for money that would hit him in the face like a bensenhurst bat in february when the first payment would be due

she pleaded with him not to do it. from thanksgiving until two days before xmas when he did it anyway. and after, she couldn't help but remind him that he had done it

but he was the father of a family of dreams. it was *his* job to create xmas. and he fought against the feeling that he was the only man in the world incapable of buying his wife and children gifts without having to borrow money. that perhaps he wasn't a man at all but a domesticated animal

and i think she understood but could only remind him that february would eventually come despite his desire to give us the experience of getting things we wanted just because we were his children and on that xmas morning, toys glistening like candy amidst the flinching lights of the tree and the december sun that skanked through the front window

on that morning i could see how her reminders and the sand balanced on his shoulders were indeed bringing him down

but she didn't.

she absently picked up her coffee cup again, brought it to her mouth. she was just about to say something. i saw it in her eyes. he knew it too, i saw him prepare for her

but when the coffee reached her lips her face collapsed and she quickly put it down. both he and i stood silent waiting for a grand admonition, something which spoke of her fear that he had jeopardized them

but instead she said quietly as she walked into the kitchen, "i'm not going to talk about this money thing again. not now, not in February, never. you made your decision, now you're just going to have to handle it yourself"

if it hadn't been for the cold cup of coffee she would have been warmed by its sweetness and put her syrupy lips to his

she would have comforted him. assured him that no one could be a better father. that gifts don't adequately convey love. that working two jobs stretched his life far enough. enough for her and us. but the cool brown liquid distracted her and she succumbed to habit and headed for the kitchen. i watched him

his face was an ineffective mask. he knew he had made a mistake. but there was so little light in their lives. and everything he did seemed small, hopeless. her silence left him empty

i heard her in the kitchen striking a safety match on the side of the stove to light the burner. i heard it whoosh

and he hunched his shoulders under the weight of the sandbags and walked to the front door

i wondered where he could go on a xmas day with so much sand on his back but he left anyway.

THE RAGGED STOCKING

by Frances E. W. Harper

Do you see this ragged stocking,
Here a rent and there a hole?
Each thread of this little stocking
Is woven around my soul.

Do you wish to hear my story?
Excuse me, the tears will start,
For the sight of this ragged stocking
Stirs the fountains of my heart.

You say that my home is happy;
To me 'tis earth's fairest place.
But its sunshine, peace and gladness
Back to this stocking I trace.

I was once a wretched drunkard;
Ah! you start and say not so;
But the dreadful depths I've sounded,
And I speak of what I know.

I was wild and very reckless
When I stood on manhood's brink,
And, joining with pleasure-seekers,
Learned to revel and drink.

Strong drink is a raging demon,
In his hands are shame and woe;
He mocketh the strength of the mighty
And bringeth strong men low.

The light of my home was darkened
By the shadow of my sin;
And want and woe unbarr'd the door,
And suffering entered in.

The streets were full one Christmas Eve,
And alive with girls and boys,
Merrily looking through windowpanes
At bright and beautiful toys.

And throngs of parents came to buy
The gifts that children prize,
And homeward trudged with happy hearts,
 The love-light in their eyes.

I thought of my little Charley,
At home in his lowly bed,
With the shadows around his life,
And in shame I bowed my head.

I entered my home a sober man,
My heart by remorse was wrung,
And there in the chimney corner,
This little stocking was hung.

Faded and worn as you see it;
To me 'tis a precious thing,
And I never gaze upon it
But unbidden tears will spring.

I began to search my pockets,
But scarcely a dime was there;
But scanty as was the pittance,
This stocking received its share.

For a longing seized upon me
To gladden the heart of my boy,
And I bought him some cakes and candy,
And added a simple toy.

Then I knelt by this little stocking
And sobbed out an earnest prayer,
And arose with strength to wrestle
And break from the tempter's snare.

And this faded, worn-out stocking,
So pitiful once to see,
Became the wedge that broke my chain,
And a blessing it brought to me.

Do you marvel then I prize it?
When each darn and seam and hole
Is linked with my soul's deliverance
From the bondage of the bowl?

And tonight my wife will tell you,
Though I've houses, gold and land,
He holds no treasure more precious
Than this stocking in my hand.

Ebony and I were going through Fort Greene Park on our way to see *Township Fever* at BAM when I was overcome by a very childish emotion. I wanted to run through the leaves and I did, knowing that my ten-year-old niece would chase me. And, as often happens when the child in me overwhelms the adult, there was an accident. Not three steps into our chase, Ebony's foot struck a rock and she flopped, facefirst, into a clump of fallen Fort Greene foliage. Happily, she wasn't hurt. Unhappily, the sleeve of her new winter coat was now smeared with dog doo-doo. I was appalled. She was amused. She giggled on the way back to my place, and giggled as I vigorously wiped the mess away and sprayed it with Right Guard. "You got dog doo-doo on my new coat," she said, quite delighted by my lack of adult omnipotence.

I was supposed to take her to see the Sesame Street show at the Garden, but when *Township Fever* opened in Brooklyn, I decided to substitute an Afrocentric cultural experience for what she really wanted to see. I'd taken her to see *The Piano Lesson,* which she'd both understood and enjoyed. But *Township Fever,* with its shifts from bright, elaborate musical numbers to long-winded sections of exposition, made her squirm. I spent much of the second act with my arm around her, trying to use fatherly affection to sustain her flagging interest. I was surprised. Unlike most young residents of planet Earth, Ebony has always preferred sedentary activities like reading books and watching television to, for example, jumping rope. Nor did speaking up in class or most other assertive pursuits interest her. It was as if there was a level of active behavior she wouldn't, or couldn't, engage in.

But that didn't mean she wasn't stubborn. That night, while dining at a local bistro, she chafed under my finicky instruction to eat her french fries with a fork. "This is not McDonald's," I said sternly. Her response was to use the fork awkwardly and roll her eyes. During the cab ride home she sat away from me, clearly pissed at a bachelor uncle's unwanted discipline.

For a while I thought that would be her last memory of me. Five days later I received an anguished message from my mother. CAT scan. Brain tumor. Down State Medical Center. Surgery. Ebony had always been sickly. But since October she hadn't put in a full week of school, and a series of intense, inexplicable headaches led her pediatrician to send her to Kings County Hospital for tests. Within hours the tumor had been found and Ebony placed in Downstate's children's ICU unit across from Kings County.

My mother, herself sidelined by a broken leg, was depressed by her inability to travel to her granddaughter's aid. Ebony's little sister Amber missed her so much that one night she slept in her bed. Ebony's mother, my sister, was relatively cool, though her calm seemed part of the same mask she often employed to distance unwanted advice— or in this case, pain. The day after the diagnosis Ebony's father stood in the hallway out- side the ICU unit, wiping away a tear. He explained that the tumor, on the left side of her head, had blocked the flow of fluid from brain to spine. Pressure from the tumor and the collected fluid was causing headaches and endangering her young life. He was teary because he'd just given permission for a tube to be inserted in her skull to siphon off the backed-up fluid. Inserted? That's the word we used instead of drilled.

Before this procedure I entered the ICU. A little Trinidadian boy was propped spread-eagle on a bed with a network of tubes and tape spread across his skinny chest. "Open-heart surgery," Ebony's father whispered. A left turn past a desk where two Caribbean nurses did paperwork. Then Ebony was in front of me, lying on her side with

WILLIAM MCKNIGHT FARROW, **PEACE**, 1924. LITHOGRAPH, 8 X 8 1/2 IN.
COURTESY CLARK ATLANTA UNIVERSITY, COLLECTION OF AFRICAN AMERICAN ART, ATLANTA, GA.

tubes stuck in both arms. Her lips were dry. Her yellow skin was pale. Her voice, when it spoke my name, was small and weary. As I stood there I could feel blood rushing into my head. Then we were ushered out as the neurosurgeon entered.

In the hallway we riffed through Ebony's life—her introspection, melancholy, ailments, and lack of confidence. Had she known all along something was wrong? Had the tumor, near the part of the brain that controls balance, made her clumsy? Had the family misinterpreted these signs for years? Back inside the ICU, a large patch of hair on the right side of her head was gone. In its place was a bandage and from under it a tube snaked into a plastic bag and into that bag ran a trickle of brownish fluid. An injection of morphine had rendered her doll-like: arms limp, eyes empty of emotion, pulse rate a crawl. As nurses and doctors filled out forms, wired and unwired tubes, and discussed work hours, I stood with eyes open and prayed. The doctors decided to operate the next day.

The operation lasted from 9:30 A.M. till 4:00 P.M. Doctors say the tumor was the size of a plum and they got 99 percent of it. A bunch of questions, including the crucial "Is it benign or malignant?" can't be answered until samples are tested. But in the short run, we know Ebony's pain has lessened and she's still with us.

Three days later most of the tubes are gone. Her mother feeds her mashed potatoes and ground-up chicken. While she moves her right arm easily, Ebony seems reluctant to use her left. This tendency is troubling, but that's a worry for another time. Her teacher, who, Ebony feels, "looks like Janet Jackson," stops by. Ebony's bookish personality has led her teacher to nickname her "the suburban girl." But on this day, a week before Christmas, Ebony is not having it. In a strong voice she says, "The suburban girl is gone. Ebony George is back and here to stay." Can't get a better present than that.

NINE HOLIDAY HAIKU
by Lenard D. Moore

1

December night—

assembling in the den

the purple bicycle

2

black dance ensemble

dances beneath mistletoe—

windsound ongoing

3

African wedding

at the Kwanzaa celebration—

the full moon rises

4

a brown-eyed woman

dusting off last year's ornaments—

shadow of a pine

5

twelve-year-old girl

thumbing through Christmas cards—

cedar-scented room

6

dreadlocked mother

in the winter homeplace

unwrapping gifts

7

Christmas Eve

an apple-stuffed stocking hangs

from the mantelpiece

8

a little girl sings

Christmas carols with her mother—

night snow falls and falls

9

on Christmas night

the progression of falling snow—

the sound of bells

It is a different Christmas... the first Christmas after someone we love has gone on to complete the final stage of his or her growth—the leavetaking from this phase of our lives—that we call death.

Christmas is a time of memories, trees, carols, decorating, joyous giving, grateful receiving, eating, and laughter. Now the person who is a part of all these memories is not present with us this Christmas.

For me, Christmas has always been the season I loved most. Oh, the decorating, the careful selection of just the "right" gift for the beloved, the warm glow of a family together, the satisfaction of seeing ordinary packages turn into beautiful creations under your fingers.

I am not alone. For me, it is my only child who is missing. Others miss their life's companion, their parents, their children, other relatives or friends. I have been dreading December. I did not feel like even hearing the carols or seeing, evidences of the season.

I know (for myself) that miracles still occur. About a week ago as I walked my favorite path, which surrounds a clear body of water, I watched the sun come bursting through the clouds and a realization that completely changed my attitude came flooding over and through me.

"Foolish child; this season is to honor the birthday of Jesus, the gift most precious. Had he not come, gone through physical sufferings and death, and risen triumphantly, you would have no hope of seeing those you love again. One day the family circle will again be complete... never again to be broken."

So, on this "first Christmas," I have been blessed to experience the miraculous revelation that I *really* have reason to celebrate Christmas.

To everyone, and especially those of us who have missing links in our chain of family and friends: Rejoice! Christmas is extra-special to us.

RICHARD MAYHEW, **BAYSIDE MEADOW**, 1995. 32 X 37 IN.
COURTESY MICHAEL ROSENFELD GALLERY, NEW YORK, NY.

CHRISTMAS LULLABY *for a* NEW-BORN CHILD

by Yvonne Gregory

"Where did I come from, Mother, and why?"
"You slipped from the hand of Morn.
A child's clear eyes have wondered why
Since the very first child was born."

"What shall I do here, Mother, and when?"
"You'll dream in a waking sleep,
Then sow your dreams in the minds of men
Till the time shall come to reap."

"What do men long for, Mother, and why?"
"They long for a star's bright rays,
And when they have glimpsed a tiny light
They follow with songs of praise."

"Where does that star shine, Mother, and when?"
"It glows in the hearts of a few.
So close your eyes, while I pray, dear child,
That the star may shine in you."

A CHRISTMAS SERMON ON PEACE (1967) | *Rev. Martin Luther King, Jr.*

✪ *Peace on earth...* This Christmas season finds us a rather bewildered human race. We have neither peace within nor peace without. Everywhere paralyzing fears harrow people by day and haunt them by night. Our world is sick with war; everywhere we turn we see its ominous possibilities. And yet, my friends, the Christmas hope for peace and goodwill toward all men can no longer be dismissed as a kind of pious dream of some utopian. If we don't have goodwill toward men in this world, we will destroy ourselves by the misuse of our own instruments and our own power. Wisdom born of experience should tell us that war is obsolete. There may have been a time when war served as a negative good by preventing the spread and growth of an evil force, but the very destructive power of modern weapons of warfare eliminates even the possibility that war may any longer serve as a negative good. And so, if we assume that life is worth living, if we assume that mankind has a right to survive, then we must find an alternative to war— and so let us this morning explore the conditions for peace. Let us this morning think anew on the meaning of that Christmas hope: "Peace on Earth, Good Will toward Men." And as we explore these conditions, I would suggest that modern man really go all out to study the meaning of nonviolence, its philosophy, and its strategy.

We have experimented with the meaning of nonviolence in our struggle for racial justice in the United States, but now the time has come for man to experiment with nonviolence in all areas of human conflict, and that means nonviolence on an international scale.

Now let me suggest first that if we are to have peace on earth, our loyalties must become ecumenical rather than sectional. Our loyalties must transcend our race, our

tribe, our class, and our nation; and this means we must develop a world perspective.
No individual can live alone; no nation can live alone, and as long as we try, the more we
are going to have war in this world. Now the judgment of God is upon us, and we must
either learn to live together as brothers or we are all going to perish together as fools.

Yes, as nations and individuals, we are interdependent. I have spoken to you before
of our visit to India some years ago. It was a marvelous experience; but I say to you this
morning that there were those depressing moments. How can one avoid being depressed
when one sees with one's own eyes evidences of millions of people going to bed hungry
at night? How can one avoid being depressed when one sees with one's own eyes thousands of people sleeping on the sidewalks at night? More than a million people sleep on
the sidewalks of Bombay every night; more than half a million sleep on the sidewalks of
Calcutta every night. They have no houses to go into. They have no beds to sleep in.
As I beheld these conditions, something within me cried out: "Can we in America stand
idly by and not be concerned?" And an answer came: "Oh, no!" and I started thinking
about the fact that right here in our country we spend millions of dollars every day to
store surplus food; and I said to myself: "I know where we can store that food free of
charge—in the wrinkled stomachs of the millions of God's children in Asia, Africa, Latin
America, and even in our own nation, who go to bed hungry at night."

It really boils down to this: that all life is interrelated. We are all caught in an
inescapable network of mutuality, tied into a single garment of destiny. Whatever affects
one directly affects all indirectly. We are made to live together because of the interrelated
structure of reality. Did you ever stop to think that you can't leave for your job in the
morning without being dependent on most of the world? You get up in the morning and
go to the bathroom and reach over for the sponge, and that's handed to you by a Pacific
Islander. You reach for a bar of soap, and that's given to you at the hands of a Frenchman.
And then you go into the kitchen to drink your coffee for the morning, and that's

WILLIAM H. JOHNSON, **MOUNT CALVARY**, C. 1944, OIL ON PAPERBOARD, 27 3/4 X 33 3/8 IN.
NATIONAL MUSEUM OF AMERICAN ART, SMITHSONIAN INSTITUTION, WASHINGTON, D.C.

poured into your cup by a South American. And maybe you want tea: that's poured into your cup by a Chinese. Or maybe you're desirous of having cocoa for breakfast, and that's poured into your cup by a West African. And then you reach over for your toast, and that's given to you at the hands of an English-speaking farmer, not to mention the baker. And before you finish eating breakfast in the morning, you've depended on more than half of the world. This is the way our universe is structured, this is its interrelated quality. We aren't going to have peace on earth until we recognize this basic fact of the interrelated structure of all reality.

Now let me say, secondly, that if we are to have peace in the world, men and nations must embrace the nonviolent affirmation that ends and means must cohere. One of the great philosophical debates of history has been over the whole question of means and ends. And there have always been those who argued that the end justifies the means, that the means really aren't important. The important thing is to get to the end, you see.

So, if you're seeking to develop a just society, they say, the important thing is to get there, and the means are really unimportant; any means will do so long as they get you there—they may be violent, they may be untruthful means; they may even be unjust means to a just end. There have been those who have argued this throughout history. But we will never have peace in the world until men everywhere recognize the ends are not cut off from means, because the means represent the ideal in the making, and the end in process, and ultimately you can't reach good ends through evil means, because the means represent the seed and the end represents the tree.

It's one of the strangest things that all the great military geniuses of the world have talked about peace. The conquerors of old who came killing in pursuit of peace, Alexander, Julius Caesar, Charlemagne, and Napoleon, were akin in seeking a peaceful world order. If you will read *Mein Kampf* closely enough, you will discover that Hitler contended that everything he did in Germany was for peace. And the leaders of the world today talk eloquently about peace. Every time we drop our bombs in North Vietnam, President Johnson talks eloquently about peace. What is the problem? They are talking about peace as a distant goal, as an end we seek, but one day we must come to see that peace is not merely a distant goal we seek, but that it is a means by which we arrive at that goal. We must pursue peaceful ends through peaceful means. All of this is saying that, in the final analysis, means and ends must cohere because the end is pre-existent in the means, and ultimately destructive means cannot bring about constructive ends.

Now let me say that the next thing we must be concerned about if we are to have peace on earth and goodwill toward men is the nonviolent affirmation of the sacredness of all human life. Every man is somebody because he is a child of God. And so when we say "Thou shalt not kill," we're really saying that human life is too sacred to be taken on the battlefields of the world. Man is more than a tiny vagary of whirling electrons or a wisp of smoke from a limitless smoldering. Man is a child of God, made in His image, and therefore must be respected as such. Until men see this everywhere, until nations see this everywhere, we will be fighting wars. One day somebody should remind us that even though there may be political and ideological differences between us, the Vietnamese are our brothers, the Russians are our brothers, the Chinese are our brothers; and one day we've got to sit down together at the table of brotherhood. But in Christ there is neither Jew nor Gentile. In Christ there is neither male nor female. In Christ there is neither Communist nor capitalist. In Christ, somehow, there is neither bound nor free. We are all one in Jesus Christ. And when we truly believe in the sacredness of human personality, we won't exploit people, we won't trample over people with the iron feet of oppression, we won't kill anybody.

There are three words for "love" in the Greek New Testament; one is the word *eros*. *Eros* is a sort of aesthetic, romantic love. Plato used to talk about it a great deal in his

HORACE PIPPIN, **HOLY MOUNTAIN III**, 1945. OIL ON CANVAS, 64.6 X 76.8 CM. HIRSHHORN MUSEUM AND SCULPTURE
GARDEN, SMITHSONIAN INSTITUTION, WASHINGTON D.C. GIFT OF JOSEPH H. HIRSHHORN, 1966.
PHOTO: LEE STALSWORTH.

dialogues, the yearning of soul for the realm of the divine. And there is and can always be something beautiful about eros, even in its expressions of romance. Some of the most beautiful love in all of the world has been expressed this way.

Then the Greek language talks about *philos,* which is another word for love, and *philos* is a kind of intimate love between personal friends. This is the kind of love you have for those people that you get along with well, and those whom you like on this level you love because you are loved.

Then the Greek language has another word for love, and that word is *agape. Agape* is more than romantic love, it is more than friendship. *Agape* is understanding, creative, redemptive goodwill toward all men. *Agape* is an overflowing love which seeks nothing in return. Theologians would say that it is the love of God operating in the human heart. When you rise to love on this level, you love all men not because you like them, not because their ways appeal to you, but you love them because God loves them. This is what Jesus meant when He said, "Love your enemies." And I'm happy that He didn't say, "Like your enemies," because there are some people that I find it pretty difficult to like. Liking is an affectionate emotion, and I can't like anybody who would bomb my home. I can't like anybody who would exploit me. I can't like anybody who would trample over me with injustices. I can't like them. I can't like anybody who threatens to kill me day in and day out. But Jesus reminds us that love is greater than liking. Love is understanding, creative, redemptive goodwill toward all men. And I think this is where we are, as a people, in our struggle for racial justice. We can't ever give up. We must work passionately and unrelentingly for first-class citizenship. We must never let up in our determination to remove every vestige of segregation and discrimination from our nation, but we shall not in the process relinquish our privilege to love.

I've seen too much hate to want to hate, myself, and I've seen hate on the faces of too many sheriffs, too many white citizens' councillors, and too many Klansmen of the South to want to hate, myself; and every time I see it, I say to myself, hate is too great a burden to bear. Somehow we must be able to stand up before our most bitter opponents and say: "We shall match your capacity to inflict suffering by our capacity to endure suffering. We will meet your physical force with soul force. Do to us what you will and we will still love you. We cannot in all good conscience obey your unjust laws and abide by the unjust system, because noncooperation with evil is as much a moral obligation as is cooperation with good, and so throw us in jail and we will still love you. Bomb our homes and threaten our children, and, as difficult as it is, we will still love you. Send your hooded perpetrators of violence into our communities at the midnight hour and drag us out on some wayside road and leave us half dead as you beat us, and we will still love you. Send your propaganda agents around the country, and make it appear that we are not fit, culturally and otherwise, for integration, and we'll still love you. But be assured that we'll wear you down by our capacity to suffer, and one day we will win our freedom. We will not only win freedom for ourselves; we will so appeal to your heart and conscience that we will win you in the process, and our victory will be a double victory."

If there is to be peace on earth and goodwill toward men, we must finally believe in the ultimate morality of the universe, and believe that all reality hinges on moral foundations. Something must remind us of this as we once again stand in the Christmas season and think of the Easter season simultaneously, for the two somehow go together. Christ came to show us the way. Men love darkness rather than the light, and they crucified Him, and there on Good Friday on the Cross it was still dark, but then Easter came, and Easter is an eternal reminder of the fact that the truth-crushed earth will rise again. Easter justifies Carlyle in saying, "No lie can live forever." And so this is our faith, as we con-tinue to hope for peace on earth and goodwill toward men; let us know that in the process we have cosmic companionship.

In 1963, on a sweltering August afternoon, we stood in Washington, D.C., and talked to the nation about many things. Toward the end of that afternoon, I tried to talk to the nation about a dream that I had had, and I must confess to you today that not long after talking about that dream I started seeing it turn into a nightmare. I remember the first time I saw that dream turn into a nightmare, just a few weeks after I had talked about it. It was when four beautiful, unoffending, innocent Negro girls were murdered in a church in Birmingham, Alabama. I watched that dream turn into a nightmare as I moved through the ghettos of the nation and saw my black brothers and sisters perishing on a lonely island of poverty in the midst of a vast ocean of material prosperity, and saw the nation doing nothing to grapple with the Negroes' problem of poverty. I saw that dream turn into a nightmare as I watched my black brothers and sisters in the midst of anger and understandable outrage, in the midst of their hurt, in the midst of their disappointment, turn to misguided riots to try to solve that problem. I saw that dream turn into a night-mare as I watched the war in Vietnam escalating, and as I saw so-called military advisers, 16,000 strong, turn into fighting soldiers, until today over 500,000 American boys are fighting on Asian soil. Yes, I am personally the victim of deferred dreams, of blasted hopes, but in spite of that I close today by saying I still have a dream, because, you know, you can't give up in life. If you lose hope, somehow you lose that vitality that keeps life moving, you lose that courage to be, that quality that helps you to go on in spite of all. And so today I still have a dream.

I have a dream that one day men will rise up and come to see that they are made to live together as brothers. I still have a dream this morning that one day every Negro in this country, every colored person in the world, will be judged on the basis of the content of his character rather than the color of his skin, and every man will respect the dignity and worth of human personality. I still have a dream today that one day the idle industries of Appalachia will be revitalized, and the empty stomachs of Mississippi will be filled, and brotherhood will be more than a few words at the end of a prayer, but rather the first order of business on every legislative agenda. I still have a dream today that one day justice will roll down like water, and righteousness like a mighty stream. I still have a dream today that in all of our state houses and city halls men will be elected to go there who will do justly and love mercy and walk humbly with their God. I still have a dream today that one day war will come to an end, that men will beat their swords into plowshares and their spears into pruning hooks, that nations will no longer rise up against nations, neither will they study war anymore. I still have a dream today that one day the lamb and the lion will lie down together and every man will sit under his own vine and fig tree and none shall be afraid. I still have a dream today that one day every valley shall be exalted and every mountain and hill will be made low, the rough places will be made smooth and the crooked places straight, and the glory of the Lord shall be revealed, and all flesh shall see it together. I still have a dream that with this faith we will be able to adjourn the councils of despair and bring new light into the dark chambers of pessimism. With this faith we will be able to speed up the day when there will be peace on earth and goodwill toward men. It will be a glorious day, the morning stars will sing together, and the sons of God will shout for joy.

CHRISTMAS GREETINGS
by Georgia Douglas Johnson

ALLAN ROHAN CRITE, **HOLY FAMILY**, 1937. LINOLEUM BLOCK PRINT,
COURTESY THE ALLAN ROHAN CRITE HOUSE MUSEUM, BOSTON, MA.

COME, BROTHERS, lift on high your voice—
The Christ is born, let us rejoice!
And for all mankind let us pray,
Forgetting wrongs upon this day.
He was despised, and so are we,
Like Him we go to Calvary;

He leads us by his bleeding hand
Through ways we may not understand.
Come, brothers, lift on high your voice—
The Christ is born, let us rejoice!
Shall we not to the whole world say—
GOD BLESS YOU! IT IS CHRISTMAS DAY!

■ If the United States were ever to be divided between schools of painting, the surrealists and their predecessors the Mexican muralists could claim California. It is significant that the capital of America's voluptuous fantasies is located within this state. Unlike the ideal Christmas depicted on Hallmark cards—a Christmas of snow and sleigh bells—in California you celebrate Christmas among cacti and palm trees.

I remember an especially odd California Christmas during which a snowstorm occurred. So rare that my neighbors on Edith Street snapped pictures of it. California Christmases are vague, because in California there's no discernible change in the weather, causing Robert Louis Burgess to pen that immortal line "seasons unseen as they pass."

If in popular song autumn is often a metaphor for middle age, winter has become a metaphor for these times. An apt image, though grim, is that of those innocent passengers of Korean Airlines Flight 007 at the bottom of the cold North Pacific—grieving relatives symbolically threw them winter clothes from a rented ship—treated like insects as they were caught in a squabble between superpowers, "two scorpions in a bottle," victims of their angry poison. We watch entertainment news horror stories about the arms race that might be extended into space, perhaps one day crowding out the North Star. It seems that a winter of the feeling is upon us and it won't go away, and because of El Niño (which some call "the Christmas child"), winters hang around longer than usual.

One can imagine ancient winter solstice men and women, thousands of years ago, praying for the winter to end and for the flowers to bloom (they liked flowers) and for the dead to go away—those who walked the long winter nights of Europe. Our reason

for placing wreaths on our doors during Christmas is similar to the reason ancient people

hung wolfsbane: to appease the dead and other creatures with supernatural powers.

Sounds more like Halloween? The seasons are similar because during the Christmas sea-

son we are encouraged to wear the mask of goodwill, to party, and to buy presents, in

what amounts to a hedonistic potlatch. Thousands of years after those early men and

women, there's still no guarantee that spring will come. We get the Christmas blues,

a pain that's hard to pinpoint, and we think that eating and drinking, and other "stress-

related" activities, will make them leave.

Since 1979, I have been attempting to read the mystery of Christmas. So far,

I have discovered that what many, including myself, dismiss as a frivolous event, cele-

brated in a country where *How to Flatten Your Stomach* is a best-seller, turns out to be a

profound puzzle of beauty and depth. What is the message in the tangled and confusing

story of the renegade and controversial Saint Nicholas, and what is the relationship

between Nicholas and Black Peter, sometimes called his "helper" and in other versions

his "master"? Why did Black Peter, introduced into Holland by the Spanish occupation,

and the antecedent of the American Santa Claus, disappear from the American version,

only to be replaced by the buffoonish, corpulent, department-store fool in the red suit

(the invention of nineteenth-century political cartoonist Thomas Nast)?

Last year I attended the Saint Nicholas festivities in Holland, which marked the

beginning of the Dutch Christmas. For hours, crowds milled about on several bridges,

until a barge carrying Saint Nicholas—bishop's hat, robe, and staff—passed under the

bridge and moved toward a dock. Starting at the ancient Saint Nicholas Church, Saint

Nicholas, mounted on a splendid white horse, began a procession through Amsterdam,

followed by Black Peter, who rode in a gray sports car from which he threw candy at the

children, who were yelling, "Pete! Pete!" It was a moving and entrancing scene, a cere-

ROBERT REID, **LANDSCAPE-BUSSEY-LE-GRAND, FRANCE**, 1992. WATERCOLOR ON ARCHES PAPER, 29 3/4 X 22 1/2 IN. COURTESY JUNE KELLY GALLERY, NEW YORK, NY.

mony I'd like to see repeated in Oakland or Berkeley, even though my Dutch friends dismissed it as commercial.

I came home to Oakland with Christmas artifacts, "evidence" that I will use in the remaining books of my Christmas trilogy, "The Terribles." Among the collection is the Dutch edition of *Playboy* carrying the amazing cover of a female model with prominent breasts dressed as Black Peter, her face smeared with blackface. The statue of Nicholas, molded from white chocolate, disintegrated during the Royal Dutch flight.

Now my house is full of Christmas objects that, in the beginning, were collected as research but have become an essential part of its ambiance. My most prized possessions include a chocolate replica of Black Peter carrying a sack—it was also his job to go down the chimney, reward the nice, and punish the naughty—given to me by poet Jerome Rothenberg's son, Matthew, and a portrait depicting Saint Nicholas standing alongside twin children in a tub. This was a gift from Professor Bob Thompson, who teaches a course called The History of the New York Mambo at Yale.

What is the message of Christmas? When one removes the distractions, the hard sell, the glitter, and the geegaw, there seem to be two: Faith is still a powerful force in human affairs, despite the jaded postmodernist disdain for sentimentality and for the maudlin; and each man, no matter how humble or obscure, can be touched by God. (Significantly, Christ was the first working-class god.) This is perhaps why Christmas has such a wide appeal, celebrated in many countries of the world. Even the "atheistic" minority that composes Russia's ruling class wouldn't dare suppress Nicholas, more popular in Russia than Marx and the traditional patron saint of the working class.

Flame–Heart

by Claude McKay

So much have I forgotten in ten years,

So much in ten brief years! I have forgot

What time the purple apples come to juice,

And what month brings the shy forget-me-not.

I have forgot the special, startling season

Of the pimento's flowering and fruiting;

What time of year the ground doves brown the fields

And fill the noonday with their curious fluting.

I have forgotten much, but still remember

The poinsettia's red, blood-red in warm December.

I still recall the honey-fever grass,

But cannot recollect the high days when

We rooted them out of the ping-wing path

To stop the mad bees in the rabbit pen.

I often try to think in what sweet month

 The languid painted ladies used to dapple

The yellow by-road mazing from the main,

Sweet with the golden threads of the rose-apple.

I have forgotten—strange—but quite remember

The poinsettia's red, blood-red in warm December.

ALMA W. THOMAS, **RED ABSTRACTION,** 1959. OIL ON CANVAS, 40 X 27 3/4 IN. NATIONAL MUSEUM OF
AMERICAN ART, SMITHSONIAN INSTITUTION, WASHINGTON, D.C. GIFT OF THE ARTIST.

What weeks, what months, what time of the mild year

 We cheated school to have our flings at tops?

What days our wine-thrilled bodies pulsed with joy

Feasting upon blackberries in the copse?

Oh some I know! I have embalmed the days,

Even the sacred moments when we played,

All innocent of passion, uncorrupt,

At noon and evening in the flame-heart's shade.

We were so happy, happy, I remember,

Beneath the poinsettia's red, in warm December.

My first memories of Christmas center in Kansas, which is the very center of our U.S.A. Christmas trees, candles, cotton snow, and pot-bellied stoves are all mixed up in these early memories. The stove is there because my first Christmas trees always stood in the corner behind the pot-bellied stove. On account of the cotton snow, we had to be careful of the stove, and of the candles on the tree. If the stove got red-hot, or the candles fell down, the cotton snow might catch on fire. The idea of snow catching on fire intrigues me to this very day. Early in life I had a love of excitement, and I always rather hoped the snow would catch on fire, but it never did.

For poor children, Santa Claus seldom lives up to expectation. I never remember finding on Christmas morning all of the things I had asked Santa Claus to bring. But always I would find at least one of the hoped-for gifts, and the surprise and happiness of that one would make up for those lacking. The big presents would always be under the tree. But hope for the missing B-B gun or the long desired cowboy suit would not be downed until the very toe of each hanging stocking was also searched. But out of the stocking would usually come mostly oranges, nuts, and hard candies. Certainly, not even Santa Claus could get an air rifle in a stocking!

Christmas without presents must be a strange Christmas indeed for an American child. But as I grew older, I learned that there are children (even in this richest of all countries) whose parents and whose Santa Claus sometimes cannot affordpresents. That year I was working in the merchant marine, and in early December we sailed out of New York harbor for Rotterdam. The boat had a new crew. Of the forty seamen aboard, none of us had ever met or worked together before. Christmas Eve we were at anchor in a strange Dutch port whose dock fronts and gabled houses were covered with the same white snow I had known in Kansas. Rotterdam's canal lights gleamed with a frosty glow as a half dozen of us took a motor launch across the harbor to the main part of the city, where we found a cozy bar. There we greeted the Christmas dawn in a warm glow of Holland gin. Back aboard ship the next day, we had chicken for Christmas dinner, but no tree, and none of the crew exchanged presents.

That was my only Christmas without giving or receiving something. Even in the Soviet Union, where I spent a Yuletide away down in the heart of Uzbekistan in Central Asia, there were presents. Some thirty or forty miles from Tashkent there was at that time a colony of American Negro cotton chemists and growers teaching the Asiatics how to raise cotton Alabama style. Among them was the late Colonel Young's son, and some others who had been teachers at Hampton and other of our Southern colleges. With their wives, they invited Bernard Powers, a Negro road engineer working in Tashkent, and myself to spend the holidays with them.

...And it was just like being back home in Kansas although we were in the ancient land of Tamerlane and Genghis Khan and the Thousand and One Nights.

Other memorable Christmases for me in foreign lands have been the Yuletides of Mexico and of France. Paris has its charming features all the year round, but Christmas there—if you live and know French people—has a heart-warming delight all its own.

In Mexico the holidays possess picturesque joys I have seen nowhere else. For nine days before Christmas there is a series of neighborhood parties each night from house to house, known as las posadas. At the posadas each guest takes a candle, and a procession is formed that goes from room to room and door to door around the patio of the house, singing:

WILLIAM H. JOHNSON, **VOLDA, WINTER**, C. 1935-36, OIL ON BURLAP, 20 1/2 X 25 1/2 IN. NATIONAL MUSEUM OF AMERICAN ART, SMITHSONIAN INSTITUTION, WASHINGTON, D.C. GIFT OF THE HARMON FOUNDATION.

Humildes peregrinos,

María, Jesús, José ...

as Mary, with her child, and her husband, Joseph, walked centuries ago seeking shelter in Bethlehem so that the Child might be born. But no door opens, so the procession moves on. The old story of man's lack of interest in his brother is acted out each night.

But each night it all ends in happiness and feasting, dancing and a party—and after nine such nights comes Christmas! Perhaps it simply means—this symbolic posada—that after the hard days, the long months (maybe even the bitter years), there comes somehow to everyone the clean white snow, the sparkling tree, the gifts, and the new birth of friendship and life that is Christmas, holiday of the newborn child.

 Early one glorious morning (aren't all mornings in Heaven glorious?) God stretched himself and began to pull back the clouds. This was God's habit every day because He wanted to watch the people as they prayed to Him.

So He parted the clouds over China, where He saw the monks chanting. God smiled to Himself and said, "Umm, that's good." Turning west toward Africa, He parted the clouds over the Red Sea. Just as He was getting ready to look down to see who was singing a wonderful song to Him in Ethiopia, God heard a voice that was very familiar. So He put the clouds back together over Ethiopia and looked north to the land of the Israelites. God parted the clouds over Jerusalem to see if He could find that familiar voice. Ah, there it is, God thought—a very clear, crisp, female voice. Even though the voice was almost drowned out by the repetitive prayers of the elderly men in a nearby temple, God could still hear the woman's wonderful prayer.

"Now, Lord," she prayed, "we're waiting, we're sitting here waiting, for that which only You can deliver, because it was You who made the promise. The promise to send a savior. We need You, Lord, we need You to send a savior now. Not one hundred years from now, but very soon, Lord. If the world's gonna be able to follow Him, He must come now, He must come now."

God could see this woman meant business. God put the clouds back together and called for His number one angel. "Gabriel, Gabriel, Gabriel, where are you? Get here this moment, or there'll be Heaven to pay!" God's thunderous voice caused rainstorms over the Atlantic and roused Gabriel from a sound sleep. The angel appeared in an instant, saying, "Lord, have I ever refused You? *Ever?* Why do You call me in such a harsh voice?"

God replied, "Gabriel, you're becoming much too sensitive." He did lower His voice, however, and the storm clouds scattered over the Atlantic. "Gabriel," said God, "I'm very curious, you know…very curious. For years I've noticed a woman, Anna, praying in the Jerusalem temple. Now, her prayers are never repetitive or boring, yet she keeps asking for the same thing—that I send the people of Jerusalem a savior. Since she's so serious, I think you should go down and investigate."

"Sure, Lord, when would You like me to go?"

"Right away, Gabriel!" With these words, God parted the clouds for a second time over the land of the Israelites and Gabriel floated down to the temple just like a feather—light as a feather and without a sound. He found himself a nice little spot in the back of the temple where he could watch and listen to the woman pray without being noticed. When he thought she had finished, he began silently to approach her.

Anna looked around suddenly and said, "Who goeth there?"

"Now surely you didn't hear me," the angel said. "I didn't make a sound!"

"No," the woman agreed, "but I can feel you."

"Turn, then, woman, and look on my face."

So, sure enough, Anna turns around and right away she gasps, "Oh! Finally God has sent someone!"

"But how did you know God sent me?" Gabriel asked.

"I've lived a long time. I'm almost eighty-four years. I think I know a messenger from God when I see one!"

"Well, ah, yes… " said Gabriel, a little taken aback.

Anna was still looking at the angel. "Surely there's some reason why you've come."

"Yes," Gabriel said. "Basically I'm here to ask you some questions." He motioned her to one of the benches in the temple. "Our Lord wants to know why you continue to request the same thing in all your prayers, that He send the Savior now. What is this all about and why have you been praying for the Savior for three years?"

Anna explained to Gabriel that for the last ten years, she had dedicated her life to prayer and fasting. It was her duty, as a prophetess, to pray on behalf of the people of Israel.

"I see," said Gabriel. "So you've decided that it's time for the Savior."

"Yes, I have," Anna said. "It's based on something that happened to me." Anna then explained to Gabriel that four years earlier, a beautiful teenage girl from the town of Nazareth came to the temple to pray. She ended up staying the whole day. At the end of the day Anna and the girl, whose name was Mary, sat and talked over tea.

"I said to her," Anna remembered, "'You've spent the whole day praying. Why are you still so sad?'

"'I'm really concerned about the world,' Mary said.

"'Concerned about the world, as young as you are?'

"'Yes. You know, I don't think people know how to live. There are lots and lots of rules about how to live, so people end up following the rules. But the most important thing, the one thing that we should all be doing, very few of us know how to do.'"

"'What is that?'" Anna asked.

"'How to love,'" Mary replied.

"I had to agree with her," Anna continued. "And then Mary said, 'You know, I think we're gonna need the Savior to teach us how to love and we will need Him soon.'" Anna turned to Gabriel and said, "This is the reason why I've been praying this same prayer day in and day out for more than three years."

"I'm impressed," Gabriel said, looking at the old woman with newfound respect.

"So when you go back and talk to the Lord, you can tell Him that I also think that Mary may very well be the one that He should choose to give birth to our Savior."

Gabriel started laughing. "Now, Anna—that is what they call you, right?—

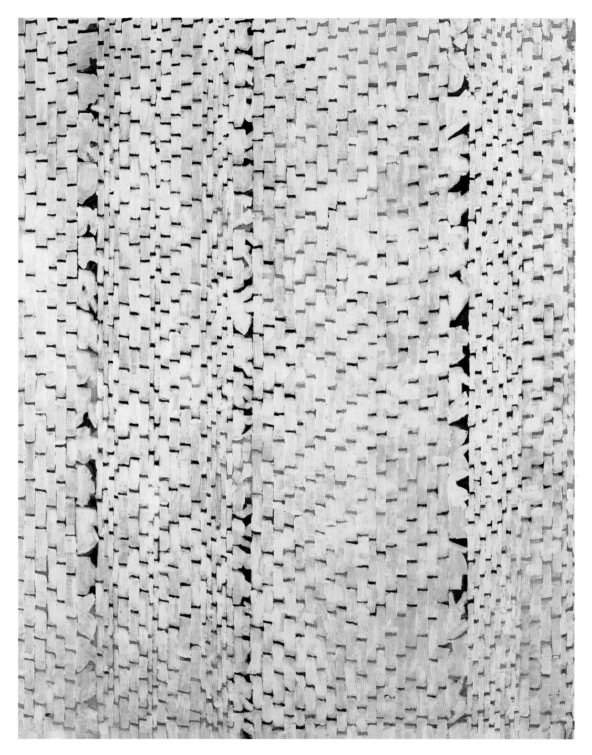

ALMA W. THOMAS, **ARBORETUM PRESENTS WHITE DOGWOOD,** 1972. ACRYLIC ON CANVAS, 68 X 55 IN.
NATIONAL MUSEUM OF AMERICAN ART, SMITHSONIAN INSTITUTION, WASHINGTON, D.C.
BEQUEST OF ALMA W. THOMAS.

you know God doesn't perform miracles on young women. When He brings forth a special person, it is always through one of the elderly, barren women. That's a miracle people can understand."

Anna nodded her head slowly and said to Gabriel, "You know, maybe it's time for a change."

Gabriel said, "Well, you try telling Him that, okay? Sometimes He can be really stubborn."

Anna replied, "Gabriel, I'm not an angel yet. Surely you, the smartest of the angels, can convince God."

Gabriel looked at her doubtfully, rose, and shook his head. "Well, I'll be on my way." As Gabriel began to ascend, he began to spin—whhhoosh—and dust began to kick up all over the place. Anna looked up and said, "Gabriel, would you please just leave and stop all this dust? I know you can fly!" At the pop of your finger, Gabriel was back in Heaven and began to look for God.

First he ran into a group of young angels. "Hey, kids, have you seen God?" But they didn't know where He was. Gabriel walked a little further where he found a group of older female angels. "Have you seen God?" he asked. And they said, "Gabriel, we don't know where He goes. We don't keep track of Him. If anybody should know, it's you!" Frustrated, Gabriel went over to God's porch, sat down, and decided to wait. Sure enough, later that night, in pops God.

"God, I've been looking all over for You!" Gabriel said. "I've got these wonderful things to tell You. Now I know why that old lady Anna, the prophetess, is always praying for the Savior!"

God said, "Not now, Gabriel, I've got things on My mind, you know. I don't feel like hearing this tonight. Can you tell Me in the morning?"

"As you wish, Lord." Gabriel left God very disappointed, because he wanted to tell God all the things Anna had told him. But when he returned in the morning, God was all ears.

When Gabriel had finished filling Him in, God said, "So Anna thinks this young woman is worthy of bringing forth the Savior?"

"That's what she says, God."

God began to pace. He stopped, looked at Gabriel, and said in His most serious voice, "Gabriel, I need you to go down to earth, yes, that's what I want you to do. Go down to earth and find this Mary—she lives in Nazareth, right? You go down to Nazareth and I want you to gather up all the information you can about her."

"Okay, God, I'll go first thing tomorrow. I'm still kind of tired from the first trip."

"Not tomorrow, Gabriel, now!" God roared, causing flooding in the Mississippi Delta. So Gabriel prepared for his second trip to earth, but this time he was going to Nazareth.

When Gabriel got to Nazareth, he asked around until he found out where Mary lived. As he approached her street, to talk to Mary's neighbors about her, Gabriel began to wonder why he should have to interview a thousand people just to find out about Mary's character. How boring, he thought. I think I'll do something more creative. I'll put her to the test myself. I'll see just how kind and generous and wise she is.

Gabriel began to chuckle to himself, and before you could wink your eye, he had transformed himself into a little boy. And just as Gabriel-as-little-boy approached the gate to Mary's house, he screamed and fell to the ground, shaking, eyes rolling to the back of his head, and began to bite his tongue. People who passed him in the street started to scream and shout, "This boy's possessed of the devil. We must kill the evil spirit!"

When Mary heard the commotion, she ran from her house, saw the boy at the gate, and realized he was having a seizure. She looked around for a stick and forced it between the boy's teeth so he wouldn't bite his tongue. She called out for a servant to bring her

HENRY OSSAWA TANNER, **ANGELS APPEARING BEFORE THE SHEPHERDS**, C. 1910.
OIL ON CANVAS, 25 5/8 X 32 IN. NATIONAL MUSEUM OF AMERICAN ART, SMITHSONIAN INSTITUTION,
WASHINGTON, D.C., GIFT OF MR. AND MRS. NORMAN B. ROBBINS.

water and a rag. The servant quickly brought them and Mary began to sing to him as she gently washed his face and arms.

Within a few minutes the boy began to calm down. Mary picked him up and carried him into her house, put him to bed, and asked a servant to make some tea. She sat quietly by the bed for the young boy to speak, but he was silent. Mary realized he must be exhausted and excused herself to prepare his tea. "The servant is taking too long; she must still be afraid of you."

Hmm, she's pretty nice, Gabriel-as-young-boy thought after Mary left the room. Most people would have tried to harm me. She didn't think I was possessed by the devil and tried to help me right away. She opened her home to me, a total stranger, and is even making tea for me herself. Gabriel quickly made himself invisible and began to think of another way to test Mary.

Still invisible, the angel lingered outside Mary's house and overheard her telling her mother, after she could not find the boy, that she was going to the market to pick up some vegetables and fruit. Gabriel had another idea. I know how I'm going to test her this time, he thought. There's no way she's gonna pass this test. With that, he hurried to the marketplace to get there before Mary.

Mary arrived at the marketplace with a young servant girl; both of them were carrying baskets. As soon as they entered, an old bent woman, very dirty, with sores all over her body, purposely bumped into Mary. Now, you and I know it's Gabriel, but Mary doesn't know this.

The elderly woman said, "Get out of the way, you thoughtless girl! Can't you see you've hurt me, you've hurt my poor arm!"

Mary apologized and said, "I'm very sorry, but I don't believe I bumped into you, ma'am. I'm sure you bumped into me."

"'Cause I got sores all over my body, you think I can't see?" the old woman screamed.

Mary apologized again and asked, "Why do you have all these sores on your body, ma'am?"

The old lady grumpily replied, "If I knew that I'd heal myself, wouldn't I? Hmph— girlie, girlie, why don't you think before you speak?"

So Mary walked away. She began to look for dates, but her mind returned again and again to the elderly woman. Finally, she gave her basket to the young servant girl and ran to a certain part of the market, where they sold healing oils and herbs. She bought a bottle of oil and some herbs and hurried out of the market and into the street to find the elderly woman. As she ran, she saw another vendor selling robes; she bought one and continued looking for the woman. At last she caught up with the old woman and touched her on the shoulder.

"What is it now?" the old woman asked angrily. "Are you gonna try to rob me?"

"No, ma'am, I have this oil," Mary said, holding the bottle up in her hand. "If you wash your body as much as you can bear and then rub on the oil with the herbs three times a day, I think you might heal." The old woman stopped and looked at Mary. "And you see this robe?" Mary continued. "Please, use this one, instead of the one you have. If you're not clean, you'll never heal." Mary then looked at the old woman and said, "Good luck, and may God bless," before hurrying back into the marketplace.

The old woman (who we know is Gabriel) was amazed. Hmm, not only was Mary not repelled by my sores, he thought; she bought me herbs and oils to heal my skin and even a new robe. But I've got one last way of testing this young woman. There's no woman alive who's not attracted to a young, handsome warrior. And— poof!—right in the middle of the busy street, Gabriel turns himself from an old woman into a warrior, very tall and handsome.

You know, the street was so busy, people coming and going on their way to the marketplace, that no one took any notice of Gabriel's transformation. The young warrior walked back to the market and began to look around for Mary.

He found her inspecting some figs and talking to the young servant girl. "Good morning, madam."

Mary said, "Good morning to you, but I'm not a madam yet. I'm engaged, but I'm not married yet."

The warrior smiled a dazzling smile and said, "Oh, then I'm a very lucky man." Mary continued walking. So the young warrior said, "I saw that wonderful gesture you made in the street back there."

"Gesture?"

"Yes, I saw you give that elderly woman oils and a new robe and try to explain to her how she could heal herself. I...thought that was wonderful. Many people would not go near her. You are a very brave young woman."

"Thank you," Mary replied. They continued to walk and soon Mary said, "Well, we're leaving now. We've finished the shopping. It's been nice talking to you."

The young warrior insisted on walking her and the servant girl home. Since she did not object, all three set out toward Mary's home. Presently, Mary asked him, "So, where are you coming from?" The young warrior grabbed the opportunity to begin to boast about all the different places he'd traveled to in the world and all the different wars he'd been in and all the different enemies he had slain.

As he talked, Mary became very sad. Finally, he quit boasting, looked at her and said, "Why do you look so strange?"

She replied, "To think that a young man as handsome as you can only talk about killing. To think that you've traveled to so many different places in the world and the only thing that you can talk about is war. I find that very sad."

The soldier said, "Would you excuse me? I have someplace to go." And off he went, running down the road. By the time he stopped at a tree to rest, he was Gabriel again. Oh my goodness, he thought, Anna is right. This young woman Mary really is remarkable! She wasn't the least bit impressed with me and surely I have not seen men as handsome as I was in this whole village of Nazareth. So he popped his finger, and in the wink of an eye he was back in Heaven.

This time God was waiting. "Well, what did you find out?"

Gabriel replied, "God, everything Anna said about Mary is true." He told God about the three different ways he had tested Mary, and how each time she had looked beyond appearances to help, advise, or guide the angel in his disguise.

God agreed that, indeed, Mary was a very special person. "In fact, Gabriel, I think you should go back down and let Anna know that we're going to take her suggestion."

Gabriel was delighted but concerned. "Whew...but not now, Lord, please. I need the rest. Maybe tomorrow?"

God said, "Okay, Gabriel, you've earned the rest. But the first thing in the morning, before Anna starts to pray, I want you to go to Jerusalem and give her the news."

Gabriel thankfully went to get some rest. And sure enough, in the wee hours of the following morning, Gabriel was there in the temple as Anna entered it to pray.

Anna could feel the angel's presence in the temple but couldn't see him because no candles had been lit. She went to the altar and lit the candles, turned, and said, "Gabriel, Gabriel, I know you are here." Gabriel came into the light and looked at Anna.

"Anna," he said, "God has decided. He has decided that young Mary will bear the Savior. He agreed that the time is now and that the person is Mary."

"Well... I see He's got a lot of sense," Anna said as she and the angel began to laugh. So they sat down in the temple and began to talk about Gabriel's testing of Mary, Anna's faith, their lives and adventures.

After they had a very relaxing talk, Gabriel stood up and said, "Well, I'd best be getting back." He looked at Anna and said, "I think I'll be seeing you again soon, won't I, Anna?"

Anna looked up at the angel and said, "I'm only eighty-four, for Heaven's sake. Won't you allow me to give the first blessings for the baby Jesus after he's born?"

"It's a deal, Anna."

JESUS IS COMING TO TOWN

After more than fourteen generations, the time had come and a brother named Jesus arrived on the scene. Many righteous folks had told of His coming to save the world, but few knew what it was all about. He was gonna be a brother whose legacy went all the way back to his kinfolk David the King. Even further, it went all the way back to Abraham, the Almighty's right-on brother.

It all went down like this.

A sister named Mary was to be married to a brother whose name was Joseph. It was Joseph, you see, who was a descendant of Abraham. It turned out that Mary was already pregnant, and Joseph wasn't happy about it—especially since the kid wasn't his.

But Joseph was a pretty cool brother. Although he coulda dissed the sister big time and had her sent away, he decided that Mary was an all right sister (although she did have a big problem). For her sake, he decided that he wasn't gonna tell everybody her business.

So while he sat and thought about just how he would send Mary away without everybody knowing what was happenin', an angel of the Almighty stood before him.

"Brother man, don't do this thing you're thinking. Believe me when I tell you, the kid Mary is carrying is a holy kid. Just like a brother named Isaiah said a long time ago, 'A virgin will get pregnant, though not by any brother, and when the kid is born His name shall be called Immanuel,' which is the name of the Almighty Hisself!"[1]

And Joseph went, "That's pretty hip." Without another word, he married the sister, Mary, and when the kid was born they called the little brother Jesus.

BROTHERS FROM THE EAST

Jesus was born in a little town called Bethlehem 'round the time this dude named Herod was king. Three wise brothers heard 'bout the little brother's birth, too, 'cuz it had been said a really righteous King of the Jews would be born. And King Herod was a bit upset about what he was hearing, especially when he considered himself the only king!

"Who is this brother ya'll talking 'bout?" he asked his boys, the big-time priests and historians.

And they told him, "Right in Bethlehem of Judea, the talk is that something big is going down. It says right here," the historians pointed out, "'Right in the heart of Bethlehem a What's Happenin' Brother will come to lead the Almighty's people.'"

Ol' Herod was slick. After he heard about this little brother, he called the wise men to him on the sly and told 'em, "Listen, go and look for the kid everybody's talkin' 'bout and let me know where he is. I, uh, wanna lay something on Him."

But the wise brothers were hipped to what was really on Herod's mind. They set out to look for the child, taking with them gifts and fine things. Following a big, bright star, they found the child and gave him gold, frankincense, and myrrh.[2] When they left, they each had a dream that told them they best be not telling ol' Herod anything. So, without a word, they took the back road home, bypassing Herod's place altogether.

---

[1] See ISAIAH, CHAPTER 7, verse 14.
[2] These were types of fragrances that made really cool incense.

But on the side of town where Joseph and his family slept, the angel of the Almighty came to Joseph in a dream.

"Hey, man. Get up. Now! You gotta get your wife and the little brother outta here. The bad ol' King Herod wants to waste the kid, so take everybody to Egypt until things cool down."

And no one had to tell Joseph twice. He was outta there in a flash. He and his family lay low in Egypt until ol' Herod was dead in his grave. And when they headed out of Egypt, it was just like a prophet named Hosea had told folks hundreds of years before: "Outta Egypt the Almighty called His son."[3] That son was none other than the little brother Jesus, the babe born in Bethlehem.

Herod really wanted to waste this little brother, and before he kicked the bucket, he wreaked some serious havoc on the little town of Bethlehem and all 'round and about those parts. He was really mad that the three brothers with the gifts had been truly wise.

"Who are they to diss me this way?" Herod roared. "I tell you what. If they ain't gonna be down with my program, we'll leave no stone unturned." And with that said, Herod ordered that every little brother under the age of two was to be wasted. And it was a drive-by night in Bethlehem as Herod wasted a lot of little brothers. It was just like a brother named Jeremiah had said long time ago: "It was a hard time in Ramah, lots of crying and moaning. Rachel cried for her kids 'cuz they was no more."[4]

And even after Herod was rotting in his grave, Joseph and his family didn't return to Bethlehem. He heard that a brother called Archelaus was running things and that brother scared him just as much as Herod had. So the Almighty told Joseph to go and be down in a little place called Galilee. And settling in the town of Nazareth, Joseph and Mary raised little Jesus.

---

[3] See HOSEA, CHAPTER 11, verse 1.
[4] See JEREMIAH, CHAPTER 31, verse 15. Ramah is another name for Bethlehem.

JAMES LESESNE WELLS, **FLIGHT INTO EGYPT,** 1930, OIL ON CANVAS, 19 1/2 X 23 1/2 IN.
COURTESY OF HAMPTON UNIVERSITY MUSEUM, HAMPTON, VA.

In the solemn silence of this Thy Holy night,
O Heavenly Father, let the Christ spirit be born anew in this our home and in this land of ours. Out of the depths of selfishness and languor and envy, let spring the spirit of humility and poverty, of gentleness and sacrifice—the eternal dawn of Peace, goodwill toward men. Let the birth-bells of God call our vain imaginings back from pomp and glory and wealth—back from the wasteful warships searching the seas— back to the lowly barnyard and the homely cradle of a yellow and despised Jew, whom the world has not yet learned to call Wonderful, Counsellor, the Mighty God, the Everlasting Father, and the Prince of Peace.

{*AMEN.*}

🎵 "Just like a Negro," said Simple, "I have waited till Christmas Eve to finish my shopping."

"You are walking rather fast," I said. "Be careful, don't slip on the ice. The way it's snowing, you can't always see it underneath the snow."

"Why do you reckon they don't clean off the sidewalks in Harlem nice like they do downtown?"

"Why do you reckon?" I asked. "But don't tell me! I don't wish to discuss race tonight, certainly not out here in the street, as cold as it is."

"Paddy's is right there in the next block," said Simple, heading steadily that way. "I am going down to 125th Street to get two rattles, one for Carlyle's baby, Third Floor Front, and one for that other cute little old baby downstairs in the Second Floor Rear. Also I aims to get a box of hard candy for my next-door neighbor that ain't got no teeth, poor Miss Amy, so she can suck it. And a green rubber bone for Trixie. Also some kind of game for Joyce to take her godchild from me during the holidays."

"It's eight o'clock already, fellow. If you've got all that to do, you'd better hurry before the stores close."

"I am hurrying. Joyce sent me out to get some sparklers for the tree. Her and her big old fat landlady and some of the other roomers in their house is putting up a Christmas tree down in the living room, and you are invited to come by and help trim it, else watch them trimming. Do you want to go?"

ELIJAH PIERCE, **THE THREE WISE MEN**, 1936. CARVED AND PAINTED WOOD RELIEF WITH GLITTER,
MOUNTED TO PAINTED BOARD WITH GLITTER AND TRACES OF GRAPHITE,
12 13/16 X 22 1/4 IN. COLUMBUS MUSEUM OF ART:
PURCHASED WITH FUNDS FROM THE ALFRED L. WILSON FUND
OF THE COLUMBUS FOUNDATION.

"When?"

"Long about midnight P.M., I'd say. Joyce is taking a nap now. When she wakes up she's promised to make some good old Christmas eggnog—if I promise not to spike it too strong. You might as well dip your cup in our bowl. Meanwhile, let's grab a quick beer here before I get on to the store. Come on inside. Man, I'm excited! I got another present for Joyce."

"What?"

"I'm not going to tell you until after Christmas. It's a surprise. But whilst I am drinking, look at this which I writ yesterday."

XMAS

I forgot to send
A card to Jennie—
But the truth about cousins is
There's too many.

I also forgot
My Uncle Joe,
But I believe I'll let
That old rascal go.

I done bought
Four boxes now.
I can't afford
No more, nohow.

So Merry Xmas,
Everybody!
Cards or no cards,
Here's HOWDY!

"That's for my Christmas card," said Simple. "Come on, let's go."

"Not bad. Even if it will be a little late, be sure you send me one," I said as we went out into the snow.

"Man, you know I can't afford to have no cards printed up. It's just jive. I likes to compose with a pencil sometimes. Truth is, come Christmas, I has feelings right up in my throat that if I was a composer, I would write me a song also, which I would sing myself. It would be a song about that black Wise Man who went to see the Baby in the Manger. I would put into it such another music as you never heard. It would be a baritone song."

"There are many songs about the Three Wise Men," I said. "Why would you single out the black one?"

"Because I am black," said Simple, "so my song would be about the black Wise Man."

"If you could write such a song, what would it say?"

"Just what the Bible says—that he saw a star, he came from the East, and he went with the other Wise Mens to Bethlehem in Judea, and bowed down before the Child in the Manger, and put his presents down there in the straw for that Baby— and it were the greatest Baby in the world, for it were Christ! That is what my song would say."

"You don't speak of the Bible very often," I said, "but when you do, you speak like a man who knew it as a child."

"My Aunt Lucy read the Bible to me all the time when I were knee high to a duck. I will never forget it. So if I wrote a Christmas song, I would write one right out of the Bible. But it would not be so much what words I would put in it as what my music would say—because I would also make up the music myself. Music explains things better than words, and everybody in all kind of languages could understand it then. My music would say everything my words couldn't put over, because there wouldn't be many words anyhow.

"The words in my song would just say a black man saw a star and followed it till he came to a stable and put his presents down. But the music would say he also laid his heart down, too—which would be my heart. It would be *my* song I would be making up. But I would make it like as if I was there myself two thousand years ago, and *I* seen the star, and *I* followed it till I come to that Child. And when I riz up from bending over that Baby in the Manger I were strong and not afraid. The end of my song would be, *Be not afraid.* That would be the end of my song."

"It sounds like a good song," I said.

"It would be the kind of song everybody could sing, old folks and young folks. And when they sing it, some folks would laugh. It would be a happy song. Other folks would cry, because—well, I don't know." Simple stopped quite still for a moment in the falling snow. "I don't know, but something about that black man and that little small Child—something about them two peoples—folks would cry."

Christmas for the Rev. Leroy was a rather sad occasion. He was called before the church committee because his behavior over the past year had been simply outrageous. He had slept with every Sister in the church, stolen from the collection plate, and even preached while under the influence of alcohol. Finally, the members of the church could stand it no longer, and a few days, before Christmas, they informed him of his dismissal.

Rev. Leroy was silent while they accused him. He looked around the gaily decorated church, at the tree, the Christmas stockings, and the like. He finally stood up, stuck out his ample chest, and began to stride up and down in front of the pulpit.

"*Yes,*" he said loudly,

"I did everything you accuse me of, *and more.*

Sure, I've slept with your wives, mothers, and daughters, stolen the little chump change from the collection plate, and had more than a few drinks. Well, you've won. I'm leaving. But one favor before I do leave.

As I walk past you down this middle aisle,

kindly notice the mistletoe

I've got pinned beneath my coattail."

WILMER JENNINGS, **DE GOOD BOOK SAYS**, CA. 1931. LINOCUT, 10 X 8 IN.
THE AMISTAD RESEARCH CENTER - TULANE UNIVERSITY, NEW ORLEANS, LA.

♫ I am one of those people who still cringe when they hear the tune "I'm Dreaming of a White Christmas." Yeah, I know, the white means snow, but there's something about the sentiment that doesn't sit well with me. That's why my holiday cards deliberately feature ethnic images, or plants. This year, I sent cards featuring either an enthusiastic black choir decked out in Christmas robes, a chiseled black wise man, or a Kwanzaa graphic. When a friend told me I'd gone too far in my attempt to politicize the holiday, I was about to agree and declare myself a victim of political correctness overkill. And then I heard about the New Jersey Santa Claus that called a little black boy a monkey.

MONKEY. That's an epithet that cuts almost as sharply as Marge Schott's six-letter N word. It is steeped in a history that allows African American people to be dealt with and treated as less than human. We were treated as animals through much of our slave history and are spoken of as animals even to this day. "Gorillas in the mist" is the expression the Los Angeles Police officers used as they left, to describe the scene of the Rodney King beating. They aren't the only folk who use animal terms loosely to describe blacks. But that it would come from a Santa Claus who is talking to a child is outrageous. It exhibits how vulnerable African Americans are to gratuitous insults, how powerless we are to protect our children from the venom that comes from fools.

Meanwhile, just a year ago, a black man sued a department store because he was not allowed to work as a Santa Claus. Public policy does not thrive on this stuff.

World decisions are not made or broken by the petty racism that surrounds the Christmas season and, indeed, all life in this country. Parents can shield their children from these silly Santas by creating their own celebrations. Or they can decline to join in a "white" Christmas and celebrate Kwanzaa instead.

I know too many people who will dismiss the Jersey Santa as an isolated incident and decide that my diatribe is paranoid, petty, and out of touch with the season. But these isolated incidents number in the thousands, and they are simply unacceptable. The persistence of this kind of racist minutiae explains the distance with which some perceive that which others call "America"—

> our flag,
>> our holidays,
> our celebrations,
>> our very existence.

At a New Jersey mall, some children got wishes, but a black child got epithets. At a Detroit intersection, Malice Green got death, while white motorists get justice. There is a connection between a name-calling Santa and a baton-wielding cop. And it's the connection that makes me cringe when I hear people sing "White Christmas."

Los Angeles, California

December 1996

Hey Now! We can't believe it's holiday time again! It seems like we just took down the Christmas lights and put away the Kwanzaa candles and here it is time to do it all over again. But we don't mind, for every time we unwrap an ornament or polish the kinara, we take time to reflect on the year's activities and count our many blessings.

The Justice family—Perris, Louise, and the twins, Ebony and Ivory—continues to grow and thrive. Perris won a big class-action suit this summer and while he can't discuss the details of the settlement, he's very proud of the fact that African Americans and other minorities in the state won't suffer the kind of humiliating redlining on home loans that we've all experienced at one time or another. Louise led the celebration festivities in a very appropriate fashion—she found a house in View Park for the family to buy! You can bet, too, when the bank saw the Justice name on that application, it just sailed on through the system without a hitch. For once Justice applies to more than "just us!"

Don't go getting the wrong idea, though; Louise has been doing a lot more than looking at houses and wallpaper patterns this year. She continues to be active on the board of the Umoja Center for Battered Families and a new Black symphony organization. That in addition to opening two new Read 'Em and Weep bookstores in the

HALE ASPACIO WOODRUFF, **LANDSCAPE WITH CONSTELLATIONS**, 1973. OIL ON CANVAS, 40 X 50 INCHES.
INDIANAPOLIS MUSEUM OF ART. MR. AND MRS. JULIUS F. PRATT FUND.

Glendale Galleria and on Rodeo Drive. Who woulda thunk it—a romance novel bookstore started by a South Central sistuh that was so successful in the 'hood that it financed two more in less than five years?! And they say Negroes don't read!

Speaking of the N word, Ebony and Ivory collaborated this fall on an essay on the terms Black folk have called ourselves over the years. Did you know the debate goes back to 1835, when a national Negro Convention recommended that Black folk remove the word "African" from the titles of our organizations and stop calling ourselves "colored" in favor of "Negro?" That's just one of a dozen different "official" names we've adopted through the years that the kids uncovered. You can see them holding their first-place awards from their school in the picture we're enclosing with this letter. As you can tell from the picture, Ivory, our Dark Prince, is getting so tall—5'3" and only eight years old! And poor Ebony is not getting any darker no matter how long she plays in the sun. Some of the kids at school called her "throwback" so much, she looked it up and used it as one of the terms in her essay, too!

No discussion of the Justice family would be complete without mentioning our growing boxer family. Samson (aka Boxer-with-an-Attitude) finally got a girlfriend, Delilah, whom we bought last Valentine's Day. They hit it off immediately, and on November 2nd, they had a litter of six puppies! Ivory wanted to name them after famous African American boxing champions, which was fine for Ali, Brown Bomber, and Jack (Johnson). But it didn't work for the all-white boxer or the two girls in the litter. So Ebony came up with Rocky (she says for white boxer Rocky Balboa, but Papa Justice reminded her that Rocky Marciano was a champion, too) and names of African queens for the girls. And don't you know Neffy (for Queen Nefertiti) and Latifah (for you-know-who) are holding their own against the fellas, too. When the boy puppies get too rambunctious, Mama Delilah slaps them back into line. The joke around here is she's been listening too much to the old LL Cool J song "Mama's Gonna Knock You Out!"

Speaking of knockouts, Louise's mother, Luzianne, is rocking and rolling with the best of them. She had her sixty-second birthday in June and took early retirement from the gas company, although she still helps Louise out at the bookstores. We can't call her "Pistol-Packin' Granny" anymore, though. She turned in her .38 special at one of those "cash for guns" programs the city sponsored and used the $75 to start karate lessons. As Miss Luzianne says, "Honey, they coulda hit me over the head any day of the week up in those stores and took my pistol, but they damn sure can't take my feet!"

Did we mention Miss Luzianne's new husband, Henry? Well, he's just about as wild as she is. They met at the Bostonian Bid Whist Society in March and have been married since September. Grandpa Henry is sixty-eight and has a number of activities he's involved in, too. The latest is a write-in campaign to get the U.S. Postal Service to issue a Black Santa Claus stamp. Crazy as it sounds, there are now Native American, Latino, and Asian write-in efforts getting started and they're calling the campaign "Christmas Knows No Color." Montel Williams even flew Grandpa Henry to New York to tape a show on the topic two weeks ago. It should air the second week in December, but check your local *TV Guide* for the exact day in your area.

Perris's sisters are doing well, too. Charlotte's still chasing the bad guys and Macon is still teaching school in Oakland. After several years of deliberation, the youngest sister, Rhodesia, changed her name to Zimbabwe. Perris's parents' habit of naming the kids after places was cool for Perris (after a small town here in California where Perris's Grandmama Cile had a house), Charlotte (where Papa Justice is from), or even Macon (Mama Justice's home). But when Papa Justice started pulling out the atlas and looking at African cities and countries, things got a little out of hand. And poor Rhodesia, who's twenty-eight now and very Afrocentric, just couldn't see being named after a white colonial regime, so the logical change was to Zimbabwe. We actually agreed with her, but since nobody has the breath to call her Zimbabwe Justice Munir, we just call her Zimbe or Z for short.

Papa Justice is still in shock from the skizillion dollars he got for his formula for a non-greasy curl activator (Mama Justice wanted to call it "Grease Relief" but that name was taken). Our new house is close by so, for the first time this year, Papa Justice and Grandpa Henry will be donning Santa Claus outfits together and playing "Christmas gif'" with the neighborhood kids. Older than Kwanzaa, the Christmas gif' tradition goes back to the Dark Days (we mean slavery—not the Reagan administration).

Back then, slaves on the plantations put little presents, a piece of fruit or some candy, in their pockets and if someone came up to them and said "Christmas gif'" first, they'd have to give them a present. Mama and Papa Justice used to do it every year with Perris and his sisters and now we're carrying the tradition on with our kids and the neighborhood children, too. By the time the grandpas get to our house, their pockets will be empty, but we're going to put a secret stash in the laundry room so they can refill and Ebony and Ivory can play.

This year will be the first Christmas for Zimbe and Jamal's new baby boy. As Afrocentric as they are, we expected names like Jamal or Kweisi, but they named him Frederick, after Frederick Douglass, which Jamal says is Afrocentric but American, too. And, honey, don't we all have our feet in both cultures?

We'll probably all be gathered around our tree late Christmas morning, wrapping paper everywhere, Ivory playing with his latest action hero, Ebony probably reading a book, Mama Justice sitting back, tapping her foot to the "Soulful Messiah" or a Johnny Mathis song, and Louise and Miz Luzianne frying up oysters, scrambling eggs, and pulling the monkey bread out of the oven for the breakfast feast. Perris swears he'll be there this time instead of at the liquor store trying to find "D" batteries for the latest gadget he's bought for the kids, but Louise will keep a plate warm for him if he forgets again. After the grandpas do their Christmas gif' thing, we'll have some cranberry cider or eggnog to toast the Christmas child and dig into Miz Luzianne's monkey bread (we've enclosed the recipe this year for those of you who keep asking for it).

On December 26th through January 1st, we celebrate Kwanzaa over at Zimbe's and Jamal's. Jamal used to be very hard line about celebrating Kwanzaa and not Christmas, but Perris told him if Jewish kids can light menorahs and get Christmas presents, too, then a kinara and a Christmas tree could certainly peacefully coexist. Jamal finally relented, so in addition to a tree they decorate with African American ornaments they

MIZ LUZIANNE'S MONKEY BREAD

8 TABLESPOONS (1 STICK) BUTTER

1 CUP MILK

1/4 CUP PLUS 1 TEASPOON SUGAR

1 TEASPOON SALT

4 1/2 TEASPOONS (2 PACKAGES) DRY YEAST

4 CUPS UNBLEACHED ALL-PURPOSE FLOUR

3 EGGS

2 TABLESPOONS VERY WARM WATER

1/2 CUP (1 STICK) BUTTER, MELTED

Heat butter, milk, 1/4 cup of sugar, and salt in a medium saucepan over a low flame until butter melts. Set aside to cool.

Mix yeast with the warm water and the teaspoon of sugar. Stir until well mixed. Add 2 cups of flour to yeast mixture. Add eggs and stir well; the dough should be lumpy.

Stir in warm milk mixture and blend until smooth.

Stir in remaining 2 cups of flour. Cover with wax paper and a towel and let rise for about one hour in a warm place, until bubbly.

After the dough rises, punch down and roll out onto a floured bread board. Cut into rounds or strips, dip in melted butter and overlap in a well-greased tube pan until it is half full (if any dough remains, form into small balls and put into a greased muffin tin for rolls).

Cover dough again and let rise about 45 minutes to one hour, or until it indents and does not spring back when touched.

About 40 to 45 minutes after placing the dough in the pan to rise, set a rack in the middle of the oven and preheat to 350 degrees.

Bake for 40–45 minutes or until golden brown.

—MAKES EIGHT GENEROUS SERVINGS—

VARIATION: Louise uses 2 cups unbleached all-purpose flour followed by 2 cups whole-wheat flour for a nuttier texture.

buy from the Museum of African American Art and Cal Afro Museum here, they have a beautiful Kwanzaa display on the dining room table. Miz Luzianne turned them on to a wonderful Louisiana woodcarver who made them a kinara that's too fierce—

it has corn and fruit carved into the base, surrounding a family that he carved from pictures Zimbe sent of she, Jamal, Frederick, and the grandparents. There's even a space for the baby they hope to adopt one day.

Every night as we gather at the Munir household for dinner, a light snack, or just a brief ceremony, we honor one of the Kwanzaa principles.

Last year we told African folk tales from a wonderful book called *Wherever Dreams Live* by Peter Harris that gives insight into the meaning of each principle.

This year Zimbe, Ebony, and Ivory have been working on stories about African American business leaders and inventors to illustrate each of the principles at the lighting of the Kwanzaa candles.

Despite the economy and upheaval here in L.A. (how many three-ring media circuses and acts of God does it take before Rodney King's words "can't we all just get along?" sink in?), we are most richly blessed. We know that the miracle of this holiday season is, amidst the hustle and bustle, remembering the love of family and friends like you. So, however you choose to spend your holidays, our love and thoughts are with you and we remain...

THE JUSTICE FAMILY

Perris

    Louise

        Ivory

    Ebony

P.S. If anyone out there wants a boxer puppy, call us ...*please!*

⭐ *Teach us, O God, in this season of approaching holiday* that we who are so used to receiving the bounty of others are missing the most of life if we do not learn the Joy of giving. We make our friends happier by giving, and happy friends are themselves the best of God's gifts. We make the world better by the gift of our service and our selves, and it is a better world that we ourselves need. So in some mystic way does God bring realization through sacrifice and this is the greatest lesson youth may learn.

{*AMEN.*}

Acts 20:31–36

"I'm sorry I'm so late," Olivia said breathlessly, shifting her shopping bag to one hand so that she was better able to hug the man waiting to greet her.

"I figured you would be," Bradley responded good-naturedly. "Looks like you bought out the store," he teased dryly.

"There were just a few more things I had to pick up."

Keeping in mind the open public area, Bradley kept his display of affection to a chaste peck on Olivia's cool lips. He inhaled with pleasure the subtlety of her perfume and began to relax in her soft enthusiastic welcome. Her brown countenance was calm and serene, in sharp contrast to his own perpetually drawn brows and air of distraction.

Olivia let her gaze wander closely over Bradley's dark masculine face and, despite his pleasant smile, knew that he had yet to leave the workday fully behind him. He relieved her of her packages even as Olivia grinned knowingly at him. With her gloved hand she used her index finger to try and smooth the frown between his brows.

Bradley's face cleared at once as he broke out into an amused and self-deprecating chuckle. "I look that bad, eh?"

He opened the door to the restaurant where they had reservations for dinner and ushered her inside and out of the frosty December air.

"You look like a man who's still thinking about that last phone call, or some letter or e-mail that didn't go out today. If you haven't solved all the problems of your office by five o'clock this afternoon, it's not going to matter for the next few days.

HALE ASPACIO WOODRUFF, **EQUINOX**. C. 1951. OIL ON CANVAS, 27 X 41 IN.
COURTESY OF MICHAEL ROSENFELD GALLERY, NEW YORK, NY.

Tomorrow is Christmas. Someone else should be on your mind," she gently reminded him, shifting her eyes heavenward.

Once inside, they were led to a table against the wall. The young black hostess was wearing a traditional African dress of patterned Okene silk that was predominantly red.

"That's a lovely outfit," Olivia complimented the woman, who waited as she and Bradley took their seats. "The red is stunning."

"Thank you. I think red stands for success and achievement. It took me hours to wrap the gele the right way." She pointed to her headcloth. "It kept coming loose and falling into my face."

"It looks good," Olivia reassured her.

"I didn't know your restaurant had an…er…Afrocentric theme," Bradley observed, sitting back as the young woman shook out their napkins and draped them across their laps.

"Oh, we don't. This is for Kwanzaa. It doesn't start until the day after Christmas, but lots of our customers celebrate it, so we try to get into the spirit, too. We started last year."

Olivia smiled at Bradley across the table. "We didn't know each other last year. This is our first time here."

The hostess handed them each a menu. "Well, if you enjoy yourselves, I hope we'll see you here together next year." She smiled graciously as she left their table.

A waiter approached their table next, wearing a red Santa cap, as were all the waiters, and sporting a ludicrous and comical mustache made of a wad of cotton.

"Ho, ho, ho, y'all," he said cheerfully. "Can I get you drinks and take your order?"

Olivia and Bradley chuckled.

"You got guts, my man." Bradley shook his head.

"Hey, it's the season to be jolly. I'm doing my part."

"And our part is to remember that when we leave the tip, is that it?"

The young man nodded with a grin. "Now you got it."

Bradley ordered a bottle of wine, and he and Olivia picked their selections for dinner.

"The holidays have officially begun," Olivia said when the waiter left them. "Now we can relax and enjoy ourselves."

"You have it easy." Bradley pursed his full lips. "When school let out this afternoon you knew you'd have the next week free."

"Not completely free. I still worry about some of the kids who may not have a Christmas because their families are too poor or not even together. Many of them are in foster care."

"And you tell me *I* worry too much...," he murmured dryly, opening his menu.

"The difference is I work with children. Our future generation, as we adults so idealistically like to say. But we're not paying them nearly enough attention, or giving them enough values. They don't have much to believe in, let alone trying to convince them to believe in themselves."

"Hey, you don't have to convince me," Bradley said in mock offense. "But the world is getting very complicated...and high-tech. It's gonna take more than just believing in themselves."

"If only we can get the kids to stick with school. But what about your plans to start your own business?"

Bradley reached across the table and took her hand. "I want to marry you, Olivia. Starting a business is iffy. I want to make sure I can support my wife and our children."

She squeezed his hand. "I don't need to be taken care of. I can contribute and we can support each other—and our children."

He grinned slowly at her. "Does that mean that we'll have one together?" he drawled.

"Sounds good to me," Olivia confirmed, letting her gaze roam lovingly over his strong chiseled features.

Bradley suspected he was smiling foolishly at Olivia. He'd known the first time he met her, at a book signing for a popular black author, that Olivia Morrison was a woman he could fall in love with. It had been more than her warm smile and quiet intelligence, her petite sensuality or charming grace. It was the way she had of believing so indomitably in herself, and in him.

Until he'd met Olivia, Bradley always thought that the idea of owning a combination bookstore and café, with room for lectures, readings, and performances, was a pipe dream. Impractical and chancy. And it was a far cry from the world he now knew as a corporate attorney, where he was making plenty of money but wasn't particularly happy.

Olivia watched the doubt in his eyes. She leaned toward him and whispered encouragingly, "Just do it."

Bradley laughed. "Nike should have hired you. You're a wonderful cheerleader for business."

She shook her head. "Nike's got Michael Jordan. You have me."

"I think I got the better deal," he murmured.

Their dinner was served and the bottle of wine uncorked and poured. They raised their glasses and looked into each other's eyes as if they were the only ones in the world. They toasted the holiday, the new year... the love and hope they felt for each other.

As they began to eat, Bradley nodded toward the shopping bag tucked behind Olivia's chair. "Last-minute shopping?"

Olivia shook her head. "My gifts are all wrapped and under the tree."
For a moment she hesitated. "But I wanted to get some other things. I had a lot of trouble
finding a black candle. And a kinara."

Bradley chewed thoughtfully before swallowing. He raised his brows at her.
"Kinara? Black candles?"

"For Kwanzaa," Olivia said smoothly, taking a quick glance at his
quizzical expression.

"Kwanzaa," he repeated somewhat blankly, then frowned at her. "You believe in that?"

"What's not to believe?"

"That's a trick question," Bradley murmured. "I want to know why you believe
in it, Olivia. It's just a made-up holiday."

"So are most of the other ones we observe during the year. They all started from
some idea, some belief that made people want to remember and honor them year after
year. Kwanzaa is one of the most harmless holidays. You're not glorifying any one
person. You're not interfering with anyone's religion. Kwanzaa is just a...celebration
of each other. Of you and me. Of black folks."

Bradley listened and nodded, but it wasn't a nod of commitment so much as it was
an indication that he was willing to hear Olivia out.

"Of course I believe that strongly. It's like breathing. Every waking hour I
function in a job I don't like, I'm believing in my ability to 'just do it,' as you say, and
not give up."

"Well, we're in agreement on that. But I believe that Kwanzaa is saying something more. Let's take joy in ourselves and our strengths. Where we've come from as
a people and where we're headed. Let's celebrate being survivors, and recognize it with
gatherings of family, food, and friends." Olivia grinned at him slyly. "I have a special
present for you."

Bradley grunted at her ploy. "You're changing the subject."

"No I'm not. I talking about a Kwanzaa gift."

"Olivia...," he began a little uncomfortably. "I'm not sure I can get into all of that Kwanzaa stuff. Why do I have to practice an unfamiliar ritual, in words and a language I don't know? Why do I have to dress in some costume?"

"Bradley," she began patiently, "it's not about what we wear. It's about how we feel about ourselves in our hearts. And there's nothing to practice. You just have to *be*."

He shook his head skeptically. "I don't know. You haven't convinced me yet. I have a present for you, too. A *Christmas* present. What's wrong with tradition?"

Olivia put her fork down and touched Bradley's hand to get his attention. She gazed deeply into his eyes. "Not a thing," she whispered. "I'm going to do Kwanzaa anyway. Maybe it's the teacher in me, but I want to experience it. I also invited some of my students to come over on the last day. I'd like you to be there. Yes, I know, I know..." She forestalled his protest. "You're very happy with Santa Claus, a tree with lights and 'Deck the halls'...but I want the kids to meet you. You're a good role model."

Bradley recognized blackmail when he heard it. But this was gentle and non-threatening. And it was very hard to say no.

"We'll see," Bradley said smoothly, suspicious of the satisfied grin on her mouth and the sparkle in her dark eyes.

Bradley waited until he had driven Olivia home before kissing her properly.

In the foyer of her two-bedroom apartment the shopping bag was set aside and their coats were removed so that there was less between them as he slipped his arms around her small body and drew her close. He could really feel her and enjoy her softness, and the way Olivia welcomed and encouraged his embrace. In the playfulness of her kiss and the pressing of her lips against his, Bradley knew that she desired him, too. He ended the kiss with a satisfied sigh and trailed several kisses to her temple.

"Where's Janine?"

Olivia slid her hands flat over his chest. She kissed him through the fabric of his shirt. "With her father. He'll bring her home tomorrow afternoon for her second Christmas of the day. She'll *love* that." Olivia chuckled.

She smiled dreamily at the sense of power and strength in Bradley, knowing that he was one of the gentlest men she'd ever known. Last March, on just their second date, he'd spent the afternoon on Rollerblades, teaching her seven-year-old daughter how to use the pair she'd gotten for her birthday. Olivia had guessed then that she could love Bradley. His ego was so intact. He wasn't afraid to look foolish, or to take a risk, or to learn something new...or to be proven wrong.

"Does she know about your plans for Kwanzaa?"

"It was her idea. She learned about it from school. My mother brought back lots of Ashante, Kente, and Ibo women's cloth from Africa when she visited last July, and she made a little outfit for Janine from some of it. She went as an African princess to her class Halloween party, but I want her to know it's not just a costume. It's a traditional and authentic garment that our African ancestors might have worn." She raised her brows pointedly at Bradley.

"If you're trying to make me feel guilty, it ain't gonna happen," he said wryly.

Olivia shook her head slowly. "Not guilt, Bradley. Pride. Is Ricca spending the holidays with you?"

He hugged Olivia loosely and sighed. "Her mother has her for Christmas this year. That's the deal. I get her after Christmas and through the New Year holiday until she has to go back to school."

Olivia murmured something in sympathy and leaned back in his arms so she could see his face. "You mean you're going to be all alone for Christmas?"

Bradley arched a brow. His mustache twitched. "That's up to you. I don't have to be. I can give you one of your gifts *tonight*," he whispered suggestively, rubbing his cheek against hers.

Olivia chuckled deep in her throat and lifted her face so he could kiss her again. "Well, we sure don't need a special occasion for *that.*"

*　*　*　*

"Daddy...what am I going to wear?"

Bradley continued to frown over the financial pages of the evening paper. "Almost anything as long as it's not short and tight," he muttered absently. "At thirteen you just need to look cute, not hot."

"*Dad-deeee...,*" Ricca whined. "You're not listening to me. I don't mean the party at Brenda's house for New Year's Eve. I'm talking about Kwanzaa at Olivia's."

Bradley slowly drew the paper down until he could peer suspiciously over the top at his daughter. He saw a skinny adolescent just beginning to show the signs of female adulthood. Budding body, coquettish tilt of the head. A pretty face of caramel tan with mouth and eyes like her mother's. Her fashionable hairstyle was constructed of dozens of attached fabricated braids. The ones around her face were gathered back into a ponytail, and the rest hung to her thin shoulders. But Bradley didn't see a teenager yet. She was still his little girl.

"I thought you were going to the movies with some friends."

She shrugged, twisting her body self-consciously. "Not if Drew Patterson is going. He's so nasty."

Bradley shuddered, but he wasn't about to ask what that meant.

"Are we going?"

"I haven't made up my mind. I certainly didn't think it was something you'd be interested in."

NANETTE CARTER, **WINDOW VIEW: A WINTER'S SCENE 11**, 1995. OIL ON CANVAS, 25 X 22 IN.
COURTESY OF ALITASH KEBEDE GALLERY, LOS ANGELES, CA.

"I am," Ricca said. "I want to see what Janine got for Christmas...."

"And what she and Olivia got for you. Now I get it."

"It's not just that," Ricca said. She slowly approached the easy chair where he sat reading. Carelessly she took the paper away and settled herself on the arm of the chair. She nestled against his arm and shoulder and put her arm around his neck. "I've never been to a Kwanzaa thing before. I learned about it—"

"In school," her father filled in. Bradley certainly had to admit that at least the school was doing its job. While he, on the other hand... "I suppose next you're going to tell me that you need something special to wear."

Ricca's eyes widened. "I can wear anything. Does this mean we can go?"

Bradley slowly grinned at his daughter. He was thinking that perhaps Kwanzaa at Olivia's was going to be more enlightening than the En Vogue concert Ricca wanted to attend with four of her girlfriends.

"We'll see," he sighed, repeating what he'd said to Olivia several nights before.

But Bradley suspected he was outnumbered and outmaneuvered.

✳   ✳   ✳   ✳

"Today is the last day of the Kwanzaa celebration," Olivia said softly as she lit the one remaining red candle. It was on the far right side of the holder called the kinara. "Today we celebrate *Imani*...or faith." She blew out the match and turned to the room. "What does that mean?"

Olivia let her eyes scan her living room. The four adolescents who were sprawled on the sofa and chair, one even sitting cross-legged on the floor, seemed uncomfortable. They had been excited and boisterous enough when they'd all first arrived together, exclaiming over the "bad chill pad" that their teacher lived in. They had been fascinated with Janine, who was outgoing and friendly and who asked them questions when they seemed too shy to say anything. Pretty soon the room had been rocking with noise and laughter.

But now they were all quiet. Even Janine had retreated to a floor pillow, where she sat quietly, playing with a game her grandparents had given her for Christmas. She looked up at her mother, her eyes suddenly bright.

"I know, Mommy. It means believing in something."

"Thank you, sweetie. Sharonda, can you add anything more about what faith means to you?"

The young girl slouched in the corner of the sofa, merely shrugged. A chubby boy seated next to her chortled and shook his head with its sprout of short dreadlocks. He made an impatient sound through his teeth. "Don't you know anything?"

Sharonda turned on him haughtily. "You didn't say nothin' either, Sean."

"When we gonna eat?" Tyrone asked from the other side of the room.

That drew laughter from everyone, and Olivia sighed in frustration. And then the doorbell rang.

"I'll get it," Janine shouted, pushing aside the game to stand up.

"That's okay...," Olivia said, waving her daughter back.

She hurried to the door and when she opened it Bradley and Ricca were standing there. They were dressed against the winter cold. Ricca had a backpack made of printed Kente cloth hanging from one shoulder.

"Hi, Olivia. Happy holidays," Ricca said first.

"Same to you, hon," Olivia said, kissing and hugging the young girl. She stood aside to let Ricca pass into the apartment before turning her attention back to Bradley.

He merely smiled warmly at her, his brown face calm. Beneath his winter coat Olivia could see he was wearing a black turtleneck sweater and black slacks. But he was also wearing a kufi, the flat-topped brimless hat made of traditional African cloth.

Olivia just stared at him because the hat was unexpected. It made Bradley look so handsome, and so regal.

"I see you're getting the hang of it," Olivia murmured warmly.

"Ricca helped me out," he confessed, touching the side of the cap.

Bradley was pleased by what he saw, too. Olivia was not dressed as the young restaurant hostess had been on Christmas Eve. Instead she was wearing black silk evening pants and a loose top of red and gold. There was no complex head wrap. Just a simple gold scarf tied like a headband with the long tails trailing over one shoulder.

"I'm so glad you came," Olivia finally voiced quietly.

Bradley bent forward and briefly kissed her mouth. "I had to. I knew this was important to you."

RICHARD MAYHEW, **PULSATION**, 1995. WATERCOLOR, 30 X 40 IN.
COURTESY MICHAEL ROSENFELD GALLERY, NEW YORK, NY.

Inside the apartment, coats were hung up and introductions were made. Janine ran over to Bradley, and he lifted her from the floor, hugged her tightly, and set her down again. Olivia saw that Ricca was dressed just like her students, in jeans, oversized sweaters, and sneakers. The first thing Ricca and Janine did was to talk about their Christmas presents. Finally, the other kids joined in the conversation.

"So," Bradley asked as he stood next to Olivia and watched the youngsters get to know one another. "How is your celebration going?"

Olivia grimaced. "Well, I think it's come to a grinding halt."

"How come?"

"I was trying to start a discussion about faith. It's the seventh principle of Kwanzaa."

"What happened?"

"Nothing," she said wryly. "They're more interested in the meal I promised."

Bradley chuckled. "That's what you get for trying to bribe them."

He caressed her shoulder and then moved into the center of the living room. The kids grew quiet, deferring to his adult presence. Bradley pointed to the T-shirts that Tyrone and Sean were wearing. One was printed with the simple French word *moi;* the other T-shirt had a screened image of Wynton Marsalis on it. Bradley sat on the edge of a chair and leaned forward, bracing his elbows on his knees. He looked at Tyrone.

"What does that mean?"

"*Me!*" Tyrone said, slapping his palm on his chest.

"Advertising yourself?"

"Yeah, man," Tyrone said proudly.

"Why?"

" 'Cause I'm cool."

Everyone laughed.

Olivia stood back, mesmerized by the smooth way Bradley had entered the youthful gathering and gained their attention.

"Tell me something about yourself, then," Bradley urged. "What's so cool about you? What about my man here with Wynton Marsalis all over his chest?"

"Sean plays the drums and he wants to have his own band like Wynton does," Sharonda offered.

"I can play the piano," Janine added.

Bradley smiled and nodded at her. "It sounds like everybody has something they can do or someone they want to be like, right?" There was a chorus of yeahs.

"I'm going to be a pilot," Ricca said.

"A pilot?" Sean exclaimed in disbelief and then cackled.

"What's so funny?" the last student, Marita, asked indignantly. "She can be whatever she wants."

"That's exactly right," Bradley agreed. "So what is it going to take to make all of you into what you want to be?"

There was silence as they glanced at each other and shrugged.

"I know," Tyrone said, gesturing with his hand. "You got to believe in yourself."

"Yeah...," everyone else agreed.

"Right. It's called...faith," Bradley added.

He turned his head to glance at Olivia. She stood smiling at him with so much love he could feel it. He gave her an imperceptible nod and winked at her.

*   *   *   *

"How did you do that?" Olivia whispered to Bradley as they watched the youngsters help themselves to the generous buffet of food spread out on the dining table.

"It was pretty easy. I appealed to their egos. Your trouble was you were acting like the teacher. This is supposed to be a celebration. They don't want a classroom lesson."

"So what do you think?"

Bradley lifted her hand and kissed the back of it. "Beautiful."

Olivia smiled at him. "Thank you. But I was talking about my students… and Kwanzaa."

"So was I. You believe in these kids and you're going to stick with them. You're giving them something they may not have had or trusted before. Pride in themselves. These kids need to know they come from strong stock. They trust you. That's faith again."

"*Imani…*"

"It's all the same thing."

"You were right, Bradley. We do this all the time."

Bradley pursed his lips thoughtfully. "Yeah, but…Kwanzaa is important, too. Just to remind us that it's not always a struggle. Sometimes we just need to chill out and enjoy who we are." He glanced at the living room where the kids were stuffing themselves with abandon.

"Hey, everybody. What do we say to Mrs. Morrison, who made all this possible?" He pointed significantly to Olivia.

"Thank you," came back the chorus.

"I'm glad you're all having a good time." Olivia smiled.

"Yeah! This is the joint!" Tyrone said.

Bradley chuckled. "I think that says it all. Just one other thing…"

"What?" Olivia asked.

He threaded his fingers with hers. "I love you. Happy Kwanzaa."

94 reasons to go home

I have run out
of safe places
to hide myself in america
out of comforting places
of brotherhood, sisterhood, and family
etched in the marrow of dry bones
I have tucked bills of small denominations
in my cleavage
felt the soft warm-cheeked whispers
of secret longing
and missing
long before last looks
at empire states' buildings,
and statues of liberties
teary eyes have dried

I have run out of safe dark deep
mysterious sacred places
of scarred knees
fingers pricked by cotton's thorns
swallowed pride
and the penetrating thirst for grapes

exploding with the omnipresence of everlasting love

I have run to meet

a present moment

more vivid in total perfection

than the buffered memories

and projections

of time

this moment calls us home

sankofa

sankofa

we fly all night together

to afrika

we fly all night together

we fly home

to safe places

privileged and plundered

the source of divine love

we fly home

chaste and naked

still

to humbly acknowledge

the continuum

of blessed assuring energy

from witnesses of the diasporean maafa

to the ancestral cradle of civilization

back and forth

we pray all the way

we pray all the way

we pray all the way sankofa

obatala tenses the neck of the brother
by dancing on the feathers of the wing
he writhes to an ancient rapchant
warrior spear and warrior drum

oya grips the lash of the sister's wide-eyed stare
her legs swallow your neck
turning your head around and back
to feel the incredulous nature of the one
who never sleeps

we pray all the way
to fend off the machinations
bite through the manipulation
we pray up our homies in the city streets
they gang up and protect us
we pray up the homeless in the streets
they roam the neighborhoods
and run interference to protect us
we pray up the money changers in the airports of dakar
we pray up market mammies in accra
fishmonger women in el mira at the foot of the slave castle
we pray up children fanning flies
in the dusty streets of kaolak
we pray all the way sankofa
let them recognize us
let them resurrect us
let them reclaim us
let us reflect each other's perseverance
like the inevitability of the rising sun of ra

I have run out of safe places
to hide my light in america
the ancestors have ignited the window of my soul
the ancestors have summoned up
a mighty roar resonating
through bodies walking between the river Nile
and the womb of the atlantic ocean
a bridge of bodies
a bridge of hearts
blowing air under my armpits
teaching me to fly
locking up my hair
resuscitating miscegenation and miseducation
the ancestors have been reincarnated
as our children
they are taking us by the hand
and leading us home
the ancestors have called me home…

✻   ✻   ✻   ✻

◈ Some memories are best left as memories. Like Christmas with family members who all try too hard to get the spirit instead of being the spirit. All the material things and all the food seem to cover a deep darkness that is so easy to judge but that you never really get over because the whole story never gets told. In a keynote address before the Association of Black Psychologists, noted psychologist Dr. Naim Akbar used the Kiswahili term *maafa* to describe the many contradictions of body, mind, and spirit which plague us as people of color in the diaspora. *Maafa* is defined as the deep suffering/catastrophe that has occurred, and continues to occur, in an effort to violate, abbreviate, and obviate who we are. According to Dr. Akbar, confrontation with the historical-level catastrophes of *maafa* is an accomplishment of our generation. He concludes that we must understand and develop the ability to face the evil and come to grips with the resultant agony.

Maybe that's why every Christmas I can remember somebody drank too much and got ugly, or some sister, cousin, niece, nephew, aunt, uncle, or mother got his or her mouth twisted around what was wrong with a gift and its giver. I could never figure out what any of these behaviors had to do with Jesus, Mary, or God.

In the fourth grade my teacher, Miss Howard, orchestrated a gift exchange she called a "Pollyanna" among the class at Christmas. We all picked names from a hat. I didn't know who the hell Pollyanna was until months later when I saw a blond, blue-eyed girl on a Disney special. I remember buying something that I wanted for myself with the five dollars my mother gave me. I figured that if I wanted it my Pollyanna would also. I was excited as I opened the box with my name on it. In the box were three Tootsie Rolls, a candy cane, and a white baby Jesus picture. The excitement melted into disbelief and disappointment as I gazed at the contents. Billy, my Pollyanna giver, had such a look of love and joy as he watched me with the gift. He looked like one of the wise men, with the North Star in his eye beaming with light. He realized the deeper meaning of the Pollyanna. I can still feel the warm gift of his sincerity that he shared with me. Our teacher played some Christmas tunes on the old record player in our classroom. None of the tunes struck me as unusual except one that I was understanding for the first time. A high tenor voice sang, *"Mother, there are three wise men at the door and one of them is black!"*

I celebrated Christmas for years and never knew Jesus. Confused by organized religion, childhood fantasies faded, adolescent self-consciousness waned, and for the first time it seemed sensible to celebrate the simple things. Good-natured giving and

sharing, seasonal changes, the completion of another year of living, the beginning
of a new year of opportunities. My noncommittal choice didn't compromise integrity
or cause contradiction. It demanded no loyalty to prescribed religion. It was empir-
ical and forthright. I was clear. But I was lonely for tradition. I swept everything out
of my soul and that didn't ring true. Then I was left with an emptiness that longed
for ritual.

The question of how to frame a viable African American family structure in
the post–civil rights diaspora weighed heavily on me and my peers. In 1972, as an
extended family member, I shared Kwanzaa with two-year-old Maisha and her parents.
Maisha, who attended a Freedom School, told me that she was going to teach *Umoja* in
our community from door to door. She was so precious. Seeing her strength at such a
young age, I planned to have a strong, conscious, and progressive family, too. Yet when
my turn came to mate and procreate in 1978, I still felt bereft of rules and traditions
of family that fit. My family was spiritual but we had no practices that demonstrated
our spiritual commitment, other than our respective work as artists. We religiously
channeled our mental, physical, and spiritual feelings into music and words that told
our stories. But we were not strong, conscious, or progressive.

We made it through Christmas 1978 unscathed because a December-born
baby filled the house with wonder and joy. Christmas 1979 we argued over what we
would do. I regressed and my husband relented. We had a Christmas tree and as many
presents as our meager income could afford. Instead of feeling filled with holiday
glee, we became somber and depressed. We were lost in dreams that were not our own.
We tried to stretch beyond our feelings of limitations and find a meaningful way to
express our own sentiments, but we couldn't find any viable examples. Caught by
the surprise of being adults without answers, we were numb. Finally, we caved in,
followed old patterns, and acted like inept replicas of our parents.

JOHN BIGGERS, **JUBILEE: GHANA HARVEST FESTIVAL, 1959-63**, TEMPERA AND ACRYLIC, 38 3/8 X 98 IN.
THE MUSEUM OF FINE ARTS, HOUSTON, TX.

In 1980, we were stronger. Malauna Ron Karenga and the US organization convened a Kwanzaa celebration at Loyola Marymount University. I put red, black, and green ribbons in my daughter's hair and we went as a family. It was wonderful! We were treated to a celebration that included lectures, African dance and drumming, and a variety of other educational and entertaining presentations. The attendees were sisters, brothers, elders, and children, most of whom were garbed in beautiful African clothing. We enjoyed the event tremendously while there, and even re-created one of the dances at home in the living room the next day. But after a week or two passed, we were right back where we had started, stuck in ritual limbo.

By 1981, Kwanzaa kicked into high gear. The baby was coloring and talking and asking all kinds of audacious questions. I had to have answers. Our home was already decked in African fabric and ornamented with African art, but I added several books about Kwanzaa, including Valerie Banks's *The Kwanzaa Coloring Book.* By December 1, our daughter taught us all of the fifty-four countries in mother Africa by coloring them and chanting them to us. The practice of Kwanzaa outlined daily rituals for us to prepare for and to celebrate our holidays. Everything was not smooth at the start as we changed from patterns of no structure or an imposed structure to our own way, but Kwanzaa grounded us. We were changed and profoundly influenced on every level of our being by the process of reaching out and connecting with our ancestry. We knew that we were on the right path for us.

We learned to name the colors red, black, and green in Kiswahili: *rangi nyekundu,* red, representing the blood of our great grandparents; *rangi nyeusi,* black, representing their faces; and *rangi kijani,* green, representing the children and their role in the future. We used a straw place mat from a Caribbean vacation for our *mkeka,* representing tradition as the foundation of family and community. A colorful ear of dried harvest corn was placed on the mat. The corn or *munindi* was a symbol for the *watoto,* children who grow up and become parents as the life cycle continues on and on. I had a variety of candleholders around the house. We used seven different ones for our *kinara,* a fitting tribute to the diversity in our family and where we came from. We lit a candle each day and celebrated each of the seven principles:

UMOJA—Unity

KUJICHAGULIA—Self-deter-mination

UJIMA—Collective Work and Responsibility

UJAMAA—Cooperative Economics

NIA—Purpose

KUUMBA—Creativity

IMANI—Faith

For us, the practice of Kwanzaa was a celebration of the first fruits of harvest time and a celebration of a new beginning for our family that was rooted in traditions that we could embrace.

Celebrating Kwanzaa over the past fifteen years has taught us more and more about our individual and collective identities. Now on the afternoon of the sixth day of Kwanzaa, *Kuumba,* we invite our family and friends to join us in a celebration. We sit in a circle and pass around the talking stick that empowers each one who holds it with speech and the rapt attention of all. Children bring their art and their feelings. Young adults bring their music and their feelings. Adults bring a variety of expressions of challenges faced and overcome. Elders bring wisdom. The circle we create is our way of getting in touch with what is sacred for us. The fact that we share makes it our personal ritual of community. Then we share food and drink and laughter.

At about 10 P.M. on that night we go to church. There we praise, witness, and testify about the power of God in our lives during the year. Everybody makes a list of what he or she wants and needs for the new year. The whole congregation's lists, which number in the thousands, are put into a silver urn, the collective's prayer pot. For the duration of the year we pray over those special prayers we make in the quiet time between the old year and the new.

The final day of Kwanzaa is *IMANI.* We begin the year with renewed faith. Black-eyed peas on the stove, cornbread in the oven, old traditions merge with new traditions to give our family a firm foundation of continuing, creative love.

Kwanzaa is also about transformation. It gives us a way to practice our strength so that our strength deepens. Kwanzaa gives us resilience that enables us to continue to work on developing our ability to understand and process our personal and collective agony. We also plug into the power source of our spirits as we practice the principles of Kwanzaa, a source eternally connected to each other and God. We choose to practice the ritual of Kwanzaa with joy, solemnity, reverence, and faith. These lessons have been taught to me by my childhood friend Billy, an original wise man, and by my daughter's coloring.

The Afrikan tradition of art is functional. Art is part of life. Life is an artful practice. Kwanzaa rituals live in my poems and in my dance. I spent Kwanzaa 1986 in Kenya and was fortunate to bring in the new year of 1987 on the Afrikan continent. I returned to Afrika in January 1994 and visited Senegal and Ghana. A refrain I learned in Afrika is "The blood that unites us is stronger than the seas that separate us." My choice to practice my own interpretation of Kwanzaa, which blends the old and the new, has brought me "a mighty long way." Clearly, we can access our core beliefs through a wonderful variety of gateways. Each of us may take a different path but we emerge renewed on the other side of isolation and alienation, reborn and connected to a thriving and vital community.

*   *   *   *

rebirth in mombassa

she came home with a light in her eyes

a month is a long time

to be away

and it is certain

by the photographs

she reluctantly shares

that she is still alive

in the pictures and that

the past has not yet visited

her vacation

the light in her eyes

she brings home

keeps asking you and telling you

how it is

the first time

you go home to find yourself

and your people

and love

it is impossible to hear

the complete story in her words

but her eyes

say she is new

and nothing will ever be the same

again...

WILLIAM MCKNIGHT FARROW, **MID WINTER CHEER**, CA. 1927. ETCHING, COURTESY DU SABLE MUSEUM OF
AFRICAN AMERICAN HISTORY, CHICAGO, IL. GIFT OF MRS. IRVIN C. MOLLISON.
PHOTO: GARRY HENDERSON.

O Thou Incarnate Word of God to man, make us this Christmas night to realize Thy truth: we are not Christians because we profess Thy name and celebrate the ceremonies and idly reiterate the prayers of the church, but only in so far as we really comprehend and follow the Christ spirit—we must be poor and not rich, meek and not proud, merciful and not oppressors, peaceful and not warlike or quarrelsome. For the sake of the righteousness of our cause we must bow to persecution and reviling, and again and again turn the stricken cheek to the striker; and above all the cause of our neighbor must be to us dearer than our own cause. This is Christianity. God help us all to be Christians.

{*AMEN.*}

MARK 1:1–7

♫ When you come from a family as high-strung as mine, holidays take on a life of their own. Due to the excitement brought on by what my grandmother used to call the high quantity of salt in the air, there was always the potential for major disasters resulting in towering rages, disappointments of mythical proportions, joy teetering perilously close to complete hysteria, and egos so exposed and inevitably battered that it took until next Christmas for things to settle down so that they could begin all over again.

It made for exciting times around the holiday table. But madness takes its toll, and by the time we gathered for a toast of New Year's eggnog, I was wary and exhausted, not sure if my Uncle Louis was still speaking to my father or if Aunt Gladys was still mad at Aunt Barbara or if my mother was mad at my grandmother yet. I remembered vowing as a child that if I ever got out into the world and could control such things, I would never allow holidays to dominate months of my life through sheer force of remembered and anticipated stress.

And I was as good as my word. When I got out on my own, I gave holidays a wide berth. I stayed home as much as I could, accepted invitations to dinner rarely, and went to the movies a lot. Better safe than sorry. I didn't even have a tree for the first three years I lived alone. I refused to cook turkey on Thanksgiving and gave presents only to my daughter and the few of my close friends who took it personally when I seemed to forget that this was a time for the exchange of gifts.

But then one year I found myself wanting to acknowledge Christmas.

ARCHIBALD J. MOTLEY, JR. **CHRISTMAS EVE**, C.1945. OIL ON CANVAS, 24 X 30 3/8 IN. DUSABLE MUSEUM
OF AFRICAN AMERICAN HISTORY, CHICAGO, IL. PHOTO: GARRY HENDERSON.

I wanted to decorate something, string a few lights, drink eggnog in front of a fire-place. But I refused … for a moment. Then I remembered that this wasn't a principle stand, it was a relief-of-stress stand, and I figured I should go with the flow. I got a Christmas tree and I liked it. A lot. So far, so good. The next year, I decided to have friends over when a bunch of us found ourselves without plans for Christmas dinner and with that weird guilt that says if anybody loved you at all you would have some-place to go for Christmas dinner. They all came and we lit candles and set a place for Nelson and held hands and said thank you. And it was the nicest Christmas dinner I've ever had. I did it last year, too, and it was even better, because we were all one year older and appreciated each other one year more.

So I had managed to wrestle my childhood memories into submission and I had Christmas back. Then I got cocky. I started looking forward to it. I wanted Thanksgiving to hurry up and come so I could buy my tree and set it up. I wanted to buy presents and wrap them and hand out candy canes and cook turkey and dress-ing and giggle in the light from the Christmas tree when it was real late with the jazz station playing all that slow music for people who still like to make love with the radio on. I was ready! But it didn't feel like Christmas yet and I was getting impatient, which is, of course, the best way to bring on stress—exactly what I was trying to avoid in the first place. I thought I had blown it and been banished back to square one.

Until this morning. I was cruising through the morning rush hour traffic, and all of a sudden Otis Redding was on the radio, singing "Merry Christmas, Baby," and his voice filled the car with such happy holiday black mannishness that I started grin-ning in spite of myself. This is the anniversary of Otis Redding's death, the deejay had told me a minute before, and it made me just a little sad, but now here he was singing

"Merry Christmas, Baby" in the kind of sweet-man voice that makes you know he's going to be that way all the way till New Year's and hold you close and drag the tree in and laugh and go to the midnight services on Christmas Eve even though that isn't usually his thing and light a candle and put his arm around your shoulder when you cry just a little because you're all there together and this year we'll set a place for Sweet Otis and all of a sudden it feels like Christmas!

So I breathed a sigh of relief that I hadn't spoiled my Christmas before it even got started good. And I sent a silent thank you to Otis, telling him Merry Christmas and asking him to give my best to the Bar-Kays, wherever they might be.

❖ Christmas will just have to hold its horses. I'm not ready. Oh yes, I know everybody is so used to my efficiency that this is shocking news. After all, I'm the one who has usually finished my shopping by late July and am ready to wrap shortly after Labor Day. Have I learned my lesson, you may ask, remembering the year I had purchased and wrapped but forgot to properly label the gifts? No. It was only minor that my father was given a lovely nightgown I had purchased in Rome and my son received a wonderful box of Cuban cigars I had legally purchased in East Berlin, though sort of illegally brought into the United States. Mommy would not have noticed the difference, since she likes checkers, if the whole computer had not come with the game. These things, after all, do happen. No. Christmas will have to wait not because I'm not capable of being ready...I have chosen not to be ready.

Let's face it. I was awake last December 26 at 5:30 A.M. anyway. We have five dogs (one for each lap, as my nephew says), and someone has to feed them. I know some folks think dogs lead cushy lives, lying around the house all day, only really working when the mailman or meter reader comes around, but I don't agree. Dogs have a hard life. How would you feel if you, once a proud canine of the wild who chased his own rabbit for dinner, who reared his children in the collective ways of the group, now found yourself with three old ladies and two boys, or rather young men, whose idea of exercise is turning over a log or two on the fireplace? How would you feel having your world restricted by a high fence with ivy winding its way down, and the cats, who once ran at the very thought of

BETYE SAAR, **WISHING FOR WINTER**, 1989. MIXED MEDIA, 40 3/4 X 19 1/4 X 2 1/4 IN.
NATIONAL MUSEUM OF AMERICAN ART, SMITHSONIAN INSTITUTION, WASHINGTON, D.C.

you, balleting along the trellis, laughing at your attempts to get your teeth into them? Now don't get me wrong, I'm not against cats, though it does seem not quite right that dogs have to be leashed and cats run free. But the real question is, How would you feel if you had no discernible reason to be? No real job to do; no place that was expecting you to show up at a certain time and perform a real function? You know how you would feel. Terrible. We know enough about people not having real jobs and how that deteriorates the personality to know that our poor dogs must feel, on most days, positively useless. Yet they forge through, keeping themselves clean and occupied days upon end, watching *Jeopardy!* and *Wheel* and an occasional murder mystery with us. Are they truly interested in these things? I doubt it, but that's their day, and they accept it with a grace we all could learn from. I am still old-fashioned and Southern enough to think living things should start their day with a hot meal, so I am always up by five-thirty to microwave their dog food with whatever scraps I can find in the fridge. My sister, by the way, worries that they will get fat and die before their time; I worry that they will be hungry and kill us before ours.

So I am up in time to make the Macy's after-Christmas sale, is my point. I could, last year, actually have been first or second in line at the door. The previous year I was in the first ten and made some wonderful purchases on wrapping paper, ornaments, Christmas cards, and an electronic pencil sharpener that also opens letters. I have chosen not to go that route again. Am I getting lazy? you may wonder. My son came home from the army to discover I had purchased a red two-seater sports car in his absence. He was both delighted and perturbed. Delighted because, after all, there is a sports car in the family; perturbed because I was not letting, or interested in letting, him drive it. He agreed one morning to go to the grocery store with me because "those bags can be mighty heavy," and as we were trying to get from our side street into the main road I prudently waited until traffic abated. "Gosh, Mom," says the now mature but still adventuresome

I've-been-in-the-army-two-years son, "you've really lost your edge." Lost my edge? Because I won't go running out into the insane, nay, suicidal driving of Virginia? "Well, I better drive back or we'll never get home." I felt my car give a shudder. I know cars aren't supposed to cry, but they do. Especially when they are purchased by little old lady poets and now know they will be given a real workout by a young man with no regard for payments, insurance, scratches … all the things that inhibit mothers from burning rubber. No. I have not lost my edge, nor am I lazy. I just have begun to think that things should be savored, slowed down, really slowly gone through, in order to be enjoyed.

I have traveled for a living most of my life. It's only been in the last few years, after my son graduated from high school, that I could actually afford a regular job with medical benefits, life insurances, and whatnot. I have learned, working a regular job with regular hours in a regular office and classroom, why you need medical benefits, however. My blood pressure, which has been low my entire life, is now up. Seeing the same people every day is really a lot of pressure, but that's another discussion. When you travel a lot you have to get ahead of things, or most assuredly you will be behind. I had to get the birthday cards out early or I would forget; I had to have Valentine's Day candy ordered for my mother or I would find myself in the only town in America that does not have express wire service. I had to have my turkey for Thanksgiving delivered and in the freezer, and quite naturally I had to have everything ready for Christmas or I would find myself on Christmas morning explaining that I meant to get to the store to pick up the wonderful gift that could not be lived without. No more.

Last year we overdosed. Everybody got everybody everything that was ever mentioned. Obscene is not too strong a word. If one more gift had come into the house, we would have needed to reinforce the floor. Did we think the world was coming to an end? Did we foresee some tragedy? I don't know, but December 26, over coffee and the lightest dollar pancakes a sister ever made, we had a discussion. Next year we would make choices.

We will have a limit on how much we can spend. Each person can only cook one dish. Is this going to be rough? You bet, because now we all have to think; now we will have to make choices. Yet that is, to me and, really, to the family, the essence of Christmas. Jesus was born to give us a choice; we humans could continue to be controlled by fate or we could accept the Savior and be redeemed. We humans may not always control the circumstances of our bodies, but we can control our souls. That's what is so nice about Christmas. I think I took it too lightly and treated the holiday as a job. Something I needed to get done by a certain time. This year my family and I are getting back to basics. We will be back to telling family stories; back to a half-empty tree with ornaments we have made over the years. The angel on top is the one I made of straws and spray-painted in the first or second grade. We're stringing popcorn and sharing it with the dogs. This Christmas will be our best ever, because we are determined to turn back to the days when it was just us, happy to be together, grateful for the love we share. I shouldn't say I'm not ready for Christmas, because I really am. I'm just not ready for the mall to start Christmas sales before the World Series has been played; I'm not ready for my favorite radio station to start the carols; I'm not ready to be told how many more shopping days are left; and I'm definitely not ready for the arguments about putting a manger scene in some city square. I am ready to slow down and be grateful for all the blessings that have been sent our way. I still like Santa Claus and will faithfully leave him some chocolate chip cookies. Only this year, I am taking the time to make them.

At Yule Tide
by William S. Braithwaite

Good friend, we met

        After many years

And many suns had set

        On a world in tears

Since the night of our feast.

        But I've not forgotten

Nor the gladness erased:

        Let Time trot in

Through the open door

        As we greet, knowing

How our glad hearts soar

        With the Yule logs glowing!

Protect us, O God, as the season of Thy festival draws near.
Give us the spirit of Peace and Joy and good-will toward men. Send us to our homes with tidings of good cheer or send the spirit of home to us here with all its warmth and blessing. Let our rest be without dissipation, our Joy without noise, and from the riot and drunkenness about us, protect, O Lord.

{*AMEN.*}

MARK 1:1–7

All of us are familiar with the scriptural passage from Isaiah 9:6 that celebrates the advent of the Christ Child, which reads:

For unto us a child is born, unto us a son is given; and the government shall be upon his shoulder; and his name is called Wonderful, Counselor, the Mighty God, the Everlasting Father, the Prince of Peace.

For nearly two thousand years, this description was assumed to apply to only one unique, divinely endowed individual. Now we understand that what we call the Christ is the very essence of all life and is therefore the ultimate Truth of our own lives. It is when this energy of infinite Love-Intelligence comes to the forefront of our awareness that we, too, can proclaim the birth of the Christ within our own being.

The Christ Presence is always within us, ready to be received by our absolute awareness of Its activity, moving through us all the time. The concept of receiving the Christ is pivotal because we cannot force the Christ consciousness to happen. It is an organic event, like the blossoming of a rose, that occurs when the light of our awareness is focused over time upon the Spirit of God within us. All of our efforts to "get" God only serve to delay the unfoldment of this natural process because we infer through such efforts that we do not already have that which is most central to us.

I'm reminded of the story of the little boy who wanted a bicycle for his birthday. All he could think about was wanting this bicycle. He prayed every night on his knees, "O God, please, I want a bicycle!" He learned the five steps of spiritual mind treatment and tried that, hoping it would get him a bicycle. He learned how to say the Hail Mary, hoping his bicycle would appear.

And he tried the "Our Father" prayer. But regardless of what he tried, nothing seemed to work. He was so desperate that he prayed, "Jesus, I've just got to have this bicycle!" Finally, he woke up in the middle of the night, took the statue of Mother Mary that his mother had placed on his dresser, wrapped it up neatly in a towel, and placed it in a drawer. Then he got on his knees and said, "Listen, Jesus. If you ever want to see your mother again, you better get me a bicycle!"

In *The Science of Mind,* Ernest Holmes explained that our experience reflects our beliefs: "What we outwardly are, and what we are to become, depends upon what we are thinking, for this is the way we are using Creative Power." Thus, when we focus the creative energy of our minds on areas in which we find ourselves wanting, this energy of want eventually condenses into experiences of lack and limitation. So when you want and want and want something so badly, just like that little boy, you are creating the idea of lack in your subjective mind. And what you will experience is *not* having the very thing that you desire.

We create a completely different energy when we are open to receive a greater awareness of our original source and essence. It is in this state of high receptivity that we find that all of our needs are automatically met, and that all events conspire to bring forth our greatest good—for this is the nature and activity of the All Good of God.

When this is our attitude, we are able to live through the ups and downs of daily existence in constant celebration of the Gift that had already been given. The Gift is the Spirit of our very life—the living Presence of the Christ within us. And it is unshaken and undiminished by anything that can occur in the world of appearances.

Though Christmas and Easter are the traditional times for celebrating the advent and resurrection of the Christ, we know that this Gift is always being given to

RICHARD MAYHEW, **SANTA CRUZ SERENADE SERIES**, 1992. PASTEL AND WATERCOLOR, 18 X 23 IN.
COURTESY ISOBEL NEAL GALLERY, CHICAGO, IL.

everyone, everywhere, moment by moment. But we can use the heightened awareness that occurs each December and springtime as an occasion to recommit ourselves to living the God-life on a daily basis. With this as our intention, the stress and strain that comes from believing we have to work hard to get what we need begins to dissipate. Because the invisible barrier of the vibration of lack, of wanting, of not having, keeps it away from us.

It is only through the vibration of the willingness to be vulnerable enough to receive, to open, that we step into the *nowness* of this moment and see that the Christ Presence, as I like to say, did not come and go two thousand years ago. We're not waiting for It to come now. Now is the appointed hour always. And we're working upon ourselves to see It clearly, to see that It is in this instant. To paraphrase John 1:12, "As many as received Him, to them gave He the power to become the Sons (and the Daughters) of God."

In order to recognize the difference between *wanting* your good and *accepting* the good that is already fully present and available within you, take a few moments to recall how it felt when you desperately wanted something you were sure would bring you happiness. Observe how this sense of urgency affected your sense of self and your feelings about your life and other people.

Sometimes, desires can overwhelm our good judgment and lead us to do or say things that we later regret. As you bring such a time to mind, remember that it does not represent your true nature. It occurred because you forgot who and what you *really* are.

If you will allow this energy of desperate longing to pass through you without fear or judgment, you can then move from there into the consciousness of being open and available to God. It is in that space that you will sense the Truth—that you are already filled with God's goodness and grace. This is the experience of the Christ: the radiant consciousness of universal wholeness, love, joy, peace, abundance, and compassion.

The dawning of this consciousness in our awareness is the birth of the Christ Presence individualized as us. We can, indeed, call it "Wonderful, Mighty Counselor and Everlasting Prince of Peace." And the Government of our Lives shall be upon Its shoulders, for this consciousness can manage Its own life—in, through, and as us—once all the agitation of wanting and fussing disappears from us. By the same token, in this state of Grace all sense of separation, desperation, hurry, lack, and limitation vanishes like a shadow of doubt disappearing in the light of Pure Spirit.

When we are open and vulnerable to receiving the Christ in the nowness of this moment, we recognize that the Christ did not come and go two thousand years ago. The Christ is not a person but that part of God in the soul of every man and woman; and now is always the time for the Christ to resurrect in our hearts through our conscious recognition of It.

By accepting and allowing the Christ to live Its life fully through us, we become part of the choir of angels who sing in joy each time another being steps into a fuller awareness of their divine inheritance. For "as many as received Him—gave He the power to be the Sons and Daughters of God."

PALMER C. HAYDEN, **TRINITY CHURCH**, N.D. OIL ON CANVAS, 26 X 20 IN.
COURTESY MUSEUM OF AFRICAN AMERICAN ART, LOS ANGELES, CA.

The Work of Christmas

by Howard Thurman

When the song of the angels is stilled,

When the star in the sky is gone,

When the kings and princes are home,

When the shepherds are back with their flock,

The work of Christmas begins:

> To FIND the lost,
>> To HEAL the broken
> To FEED the hungry
>> To RELEASE the prisoner
> To REBUILD nations
>> To BRING PEACE among brothers

To MAKE MUSIC in the heart.

EDWARD M. BANNISTER (1828–1901) was born in St. Andrews, New Brunswick, Canada, and settled in Boston, where he studied at Lowell Institute before moving to Providence, Rhode Island. In 1876, Bannister was awarded the first-place bronze medal at the Philadelphia Centennial for his painting *Under the Oaks,* the first African American to win a national art award. During his lifetime, Bannister was a prominent member of social and artistic circles in Boston and Providence, Rhode Island, where he was a founding member of the Providence Art Club. His landscapes reflected the influence of the Hudson River School and the Barbizon School.

MICHAEL BECKWITH is the founding minister of Agape Church of Religious Science in Santa Monica, California. His sermon "Receiving the Christ" was originally given in 1992.

JOHN BIGGERS was born in Gastonia, North Carolina, studied at Hampton University and Pennsylvania State University, and enjoyed a distinguished teaching career at Texas Southern University. In 1957, he made the first of many trips to Africa to study the continent's cultures, traditions, and art. His work has been exhibited in solo and group shows for over fifty years, including the Museum of Modern Art's 1943 landmark exhibition *Young Negro Art;* Atlanta University's show of 1944, *Two Centuries of Black American Art;* and the current retrospective *The Art of John Biggers: View from the Upper Room.*

WILLIAM S. BRAITHWAITE (1878–1962) was a major advocate of American poetry and one of the first African American literary critics. A poet in his own right, Braithwaite was probably better known as the editor of volumes of Elizabethan, Georgian, and Restoration verse, for his biographies of the Brontës, and as the influential editor of *The Anthology of Magazine Verse* and *The Yearbook of American Poetry.*

ROSCOE CONKLIN BRUCE (1879–1950) was the son of Senator Blanche Kelso Bruce, the first African American to be elected to the U.S. Senate. A Phi Beta Kappa graduate of Harvard College, Bruce was director of the Academic Department at Tuskegee, a leading educator, and superintendent of schools for the Washington, D.C. public school system's tenth division.

DANELLA CARTER is a fiction and food writer living in upstate New York. She is the author of *Down Home Wholesome: 300 Low-Fat Recipes from a New Soul Kitchen.* She is completing a short story collection, *Pop Incognito,* and *Quasi Plus Two,* a novel.

NANNETTE CARTER graduated from Oberlin College and Pratt Institute of Art. Her works have been exhibited widely in the U.S., including several solo exhibitions and group exhibitions at the National Museum of Women in the Arts, the Studio Museum in Harlem, and the Newark Museum's *Twentieth-Century Afro-American Artists.* Carter's selected works were also included in the group exhibition *Prints from the Bob Blackburn Printmaking Workshop,* which toured West Africa.

LEAH CHASE is a master chef who specializes in Creole cooking. She is the creative force behind the family-owned Dooky Chase's Restaurant in New Orleans, where she has worked and cooked for fifty years. Chase is the author of *The Dooky Chase Cookbook* and was profiled in the book *I Dream a World.*

ALBERT CHONG was born in Kingston, Jamaica, of African and Chinese ancestry. He attended the School of Visual Arts in New York and the University of California at San Diego before accepting a faculty appointment in the Department of Fine Arts at the University of Colorado at Boulder. His work has been exhibited nationally and internationally, including at the Ansel Adams Center for Photography, the First Johannesburg Biennial in South Africa, and in *Imagining Families: Images and Voices* at the National African American Museum Project of the Smithsonian Institution.

PATRICK CLARK began his culinary training at New York City Technical College as well as in England and France, where he apprenticed with Michel Guérard at Les Prés et Sources d'Eugénie in Les Bains. He opened his own restaurant, Metro, and was executive chef at Odeon and Café Luxembourg in New York City and the Hay-Adams Hotel in Washington, D.C. Returning to New York City, he became executive chef of Tavern on the Green. He has been a featured chef in Julia Child's *Cooking with Master Chefs* and *The Artist's Table,* and is presently completing his own cookbook.

PEARL CLEAGE is a playwright and author who resides in Atlanta, Georgia. Among her plays are *puppetplay, Good News,* and *Hospice.* Her collected writings include *One for the Brothers, The Brass Bed and Other Stories, Mad at Miles,* and *Deals with the Devil.*

ALLAN ROHAN CRITE was born in 1910 in Plainfield, New Jersey, and studied at the Massachusetts School of Art and the Boston Museum of Fine Arts. Although he is best known for his paintings of street scenes of African Americans, Crite has painted equally compelling religious subjects. His black-and-white drawings were published in a series of books in the 1940s, including *Three Spirituals from Earth to Heaven* (1948). His work has been exhibited in numerous solo and group shows, among them *Against the Odds: African-American Artists and the Harmon Foundation.*

DARYL CUMBER DANCE is the author of *Shuckin' and Jivin': Folklore from Contemporary Black Americans; Folklore from Contemporary Jamaicans;* and *Long Gone: The Mecklenburg Six and the Theme of Escape in Black Folklore.* A professor of English at Virginia Commonwealth University, she is the editor of *Fifty Caribbean Writers: A Bio-Bibliographical and Critical Sourcebook.*

TOI DERRICOTTE, born in Detroit, has published three poetry collections, *Natural Birth, The Empress of the Death House,* and *Captivity,* and is the recipient of numerous honors and awards. She is currently associate professor of English at the University of Pittsburgh and lives in Potomac, Maryland, with her husband and son.

AARON DOUGLAS (1899–1979), born in Topeka, Kansas, was a world-renowned painter and muralist most active during the Harlem Renaissance. Douglas's work embraced the African ancestral arts and expressed a pride in the African American image that was highly controversial for its time. His illustrations were featured on the cover of *Opportunity* magazine and in the books such as *Caroling Dusk and God's Trombone,* while his paintings are collected by private individuals and Hampton University Art Museum, Fisk University Art Museum, and Amistad Research Center, among others.

RITA DOVE was born in Akron, Ohio, and educated at Miami University of Ohio, Universität Tübingen in Germany, and the University of Iowa. Among her poetry collections are *The Yellow House on the Corner, Museum, Thomas and Beulah, Grace Notes,* and *Mother Love.* In addition to the Pulitzer Prize she received in 1987 for *Thomas and Beulah,* she served from 1993 to 1995 as Poet Laureate of the United States and Consultant in

Poetry at the Library of Congress. Currently Commonwealth Professor of English at the University of Virginia, Dove lives near Charlottesville with her husband and daughter.

W. E. B. DU BOIS (1868–1963) was born in Great Barrington, Massachusetts. One of America's most outstanding and prolific men of letters, Du Bois was one of the founders of the NAACP and founder and editor of *The Crisis.* He was the author of several works of fiction and nonfiction, including *The Souls of Black Folks, The Quest of the Silver Fleece,* and *Dark Princess.*

NANCY J. FAIRLEY is an anthropologist who has conducted fieldwork in Central Africa, the Caribbean, and the southern United States. She is presently a professor at Davidson College and director of both the Ethnic Studies Program and the West Africa Study Abroad Program. She credits her daughter with stimulating her interest in storytelling.

WILLIAM MCKNIGHT FARROW (1885–1967) attended The School of the Art Institute of Chicago and was an active member of the Chicago art community. His lithographs and etchings, among them *Ringling House* and *Peace,* were part of a line of Christmas cards he designed for his own company in the mid-1920s. In 1933, *Peace* was selected among the fifty best American prints by the American Art Dealers Association.

JESSIE REDMON FAUSET (1882-1961) was an editor, poet, and novelist of the Harlem Renaissance. She is best known as the literary editor of *The Crisis* and *The Brownie's Book,* for the poem "La Vie C'est la Vie," and for the novels *There Is Confusion, Plum Bun, The Chinaberry Tree,* and *Comedy: American Style.*

CAROL FREEMAN was born in Rayville, Louisiana, attended Oakland City College and the University of California at Berkeley, and described herself philosophically as a "revolutionary black nationalist." Her poem "Gift" was anthologized in Langston Hughes and Arna Bontemps's collection *The Poetry of the Negro* and in *Black Fire,* edited by Amiri Baraka and Larry Neal.

NELSON GEORGE is the author of several nonfiction books, including *Blackface; Buppies, B-Boys, Baps and Bohos;* and *Elevating the Game,* and the novels *Urban Romance* and *Seduced: The Life and Times of a One-Hit Wonder.*

NIKKI GIOVANNI was born in Knoxville, Tennessee. She is a writer and poet whose poetry collections include *Black Feeling, Black Talk, Black Judgement,* as well as *My House, The Women and the Men, Cotton Candy on a Rainy Day,* and *Those Who Ride the Night Wind.* She is also the author of the essay collections *Sacred Cows...And Other Edibles and Racism 101,* as well as editor of the anthology *Grand/Mothers* and *Night Comes Softly (Anthology of Black Female Voices).*

YVONNE GREGORY was born in 1919 and attended Fisk University, where she contributed poems to the *Fisk Herald.* Her poem "Lullaby for a Newborn Baby" was anthologized in *American Negro Poetry,* a 1963 collection edited by Arna Bontemps.

ANGELINA WELD GRIMKÉ (1880–1958) was a teacher, poet, and one of the first African American playwrights. She was best known for the play *Rachel* (1916), which deals with lynching, and the short story "The Closing Door" (1919), which appeared in Margaret Sanger's *Birth Control Review.* While most of her work appeared in *Crisis* and *Opportunity* magazines, her work was published posthumously in 1991 in *Selected Works of Angelina Weld Grimké,* her only major book.

FRANCES ELLEN WATKINS HARPER (1825–1911) was a notable poet, novelist, and abolitionist and the best-known black poet prior to the emergence of Paul Laurence Dunbar. Recognized for her poetry volumes *Poems on Miscellaneous Subjects* (1854) and *Moses: A Story of the Nile* (1869), she was also the author of *Iola Leroy, or Shadows Uplifted* (1892), the second of only a few novels by black women written in the nineteenth century, and "The Two Offers" (1859), the first short story published by an African American writer. In addition to her work as an author, Harper was in the vanguard of the radical black and women's movements, lectured extensively for the antislavery movement, and was a founding member of the National Council of Negro Women.

PALMER HAYDEN (1890–1973) was the pseudonym of Peyton Cole Hedgeman, who was born in Widewater, Virginia. A World War I veteran who worked as a letter carrier and janitor while pursuing art classes at night, Hayden was launched on his career in 1926 when he won the first-prize gold medal in the initial Harmon Foundation awards. Hayden would later adopt a "consciously naive" style that was expressed most impressively in his twelve-painting series, *The Ballad of John Henry,* begun in 1944. Hayden's work has been represented in major solo and group exhibitions, including *The Evolution of the Afro-American Artist* and *Two Centuries of Black American Art.*

LESLIE PINCKNEY HILL (1880–1960) was a poet, dramatist, and educator whose works included the poetry collection *Wings of Oppression* (1927) and the play *Toussaint L'Ouverture: A Dramatic History* (1928). "Christmas at Melrose," one of his best-known poems, was a tribute to his wife, Jane, and six children. It was anthologized in James Weldon Johnson's 1922 collection, *The Book of American Negro Poetry.* Hill also served as president of Cheyney State College and administrator of Mercy-Douglass Hospital in Philadelphia.

LANGSTON HUGHES (1902–1967) was born in Joplin, Missouri. A major writer of the Harlem Renaissance, who was best known for his poetry and short stories, Hughes was also a columnist, playwright, juvenile author, editor of eight anthologies, and author of the autobiographical *The Big Sea.* His stories featuring Jesse B. Simple are collected in *The Best of Simple* and *The Return of Simple.*

EUNICE ROBERTA HUNTON (Later CARTER) (1899–1970) was an attorney, club woman, social activist, and writer whose fiction and book reviews appeared exclusively in *Opportunity* magazine.

HARRIET JACOBS was born into slavery around 1813 in Edenton, North Carolina. Sexually harassed by the father of her three-year-old mistress, she became involved with a young white lawyer, whose two children she bore. In 1835, after her master threatened her with work on the plantation unless she submitted sexually, Jacobs ran away and later went into hiding. In 1842, she escaped north to Brooklyn. Her account of her life, *Incidents in the Life of a Slave Girl,* was originally published in 1861 under the pseudonym Linda Brent.

WILMER A. JENNINGS (1910–1991), born in Atlanta, graduated from Morehouse College in 1931 and was a student of Hale Woodruff for several years. Jennings worked in the Public Works of Art Project and the Works Progress Administration (WPA) before attending the Rhode Island School of Design. Although best known as a painter and printmaker, Jennings was also a designer of stage sets and jewelry. Jennings's painting *Portrait of Ernestine E. Brazeal* is believed to have been painted while he was a student at Morehouse.

GEORGIA DOUGLAS JOHNSON (1877–1966) was among the best-known women writers of the Harlem Renaissance. Her poems, short stories, and plays appeared in the major Negro periodicals of the era although she is best known for the poetry volumes *The Heart of a Woman* (1918) and *An Autumn Love Cycle* (1928).

IMANI CONSTANCE JOHNSON-BURNETT is founder and director of Sisters in Divine Order, a self-help collective, and their Word-of-Mouth Band (WOMB), a performance artwork in progress. Her writing has appeared in *My Soul Is a Witness: African American Women's Spirituality,* and her publications include a collection of short stories and poems entitled *Soul Kiss.*

WILLIAM H. JOHNSON (1901–1970) was one of the most notable and tragic African American painters of the early twentieth century. Born in Florence, South Carolina, Johnson traveled to New York, Province-town, and later Europe to study painting. He painted in a variety of media and styles, including Impressionism, Cubism, Fauvism, German Expressionism, and a consciously naive manner. A recipient of the Harmon Foundation's gold medal, Johnson was represented in major group and solo exhibitions before a mental breakdown in 1947 and death from acute pancreatitis in 1970.

ARNOLD J. KEMP is a visual artist and writer who has exhibited his drawings, sculptures, and installations in the U.S. and abroad. His poetry has been published in *Three Rivers Poetry Journal, Calalloo, Agni Review,* and *Mirage,* and was included in the anthology *On the Verge.* A graduate of Tufts University and the School of the Museum of Fine Arts in Boston, Mr. Kemp lives in San Francisco.

MARTIN LUTHER KING, JR. (1929–1968) was born in Atlanta and became a leading figure in the U.S. civil rights movement, beginning with his leadership during the 1955–1956 Montgomery, Alabama, bus boy-cott, which was sparked by Rosa Parks's refusal to surrender her seat to a white man on a segregated bus. A recipient of the Nobel Peace Prize in 1964 for his work, King delivered "A Christmas Sermon on Peace" at Ebenezer Baptist Church in 1967, less than four months before his assassination in Memphis, Tennessee, on April 4, 1968.

SANDRA KITT, with fifteen published books, is considered to be the foremost African American writer of romance novels. Her most recent novels include *Serenade, Sincerely, The Color of Love,* and *Significant Others.* A native of New York City, she is the Manager of Library Services at the American Museum–Hayden Planetarium and has worked as a graphic designer and an illustrator.

HUGHIE LEE-SMITH was born in Eustis, Florida. After studying at the Cleveland Institute of Art, Wayne State University, and elsewhere, Lee-Smith began an artistic career that has garnered him acclaim as a master of social realism, surrealism, and romantic realism. His work has been collected by individuals, corporations, and museums, including the Detroit Institute of Art, the New Jersey State Museum, and the Schomburg Center for Research in Black Culture.

EDNA LEWIS is the author of *In the Pursuit of Flavor* and *The Taste of Country Cooking.* She has been a guest chef at Hubert's and Dean & Deluca in New York City, at Fearrington House in Chapel Hill, North Carolina, and at Mondavi Vineyards' The Great Chefs of France cooking school in California. Her menus and recipes have been featured in a variety of publications, including *Gourmet, Redbook,* and *Food & Wine.*

FELIX H. LIDDELL is the coauthor of *I, Too, Sing America: The African-American Book of Days* and coeditor of *I Hear a Symphony: African Americans Celebrate Love,* which won the Black Caucus of the American Library Association's Fiction Honors and PEN Oakland's Josephine Miles Award for multicultural literature. He is also cofounder of Livre Noir, a book packaging and consulting firm located in Los Angeles.

JULIANNE MALVEAUX is an economist, a commentator on the PBS television program *To the Contrary,* a syndicated columnist, and the author of *Sex, Lies and Stereotypes.*

CLARENCE MAJOR is the author of seven novels and nine books of poetry. He has also compiled *Juba to Jive: A Dictionary of African-American Slang* and edited *Calling the Wind: Twentieth-Century African American Short Stories.* His work has been translated into several languages and he was the subject of two special issues of *African-American Review.* He is currently professor of African-American Literature and Creative Writing, University of California, Davis.

RICHARD MAYHEW was born in Amityville, New York, and studied art at the Art Students League, Columbia University, and the Accademia in Florence, Italy. A revolutionary and well-respected landscape artist, Mayhew was a contemporary of artists like Romare Bearden, Charles Alston, and Hale Woodruff and formed with them Spiral, a forum for artistic innovation and exploration of the African American artist's relationship to the civil rights movement.

P. K. MCCARY is a journalist, lecturer, and stage artist. Her books *The Black Bible Chronicles: From Genesis to the Promised Land* and *The Black Bible Chronicles: Rappin' with Jesus* present a revisioning of the Old and New Testaments into modern-day urban language. *The Black Bible Chronicles* are presently being developed for the stage.

CLAUDE MCKAY (1889–1948) was born in Clarendon, Jamaica, and emigrated to the United States in 1912. His poetry was collected in volumes such as *Harlem Shadows* and his novels included *Home to Harlem* and *Banjo.*

LENARD D. MOORE is the author of several volumes of poetry, including *Forever Home.* His poems, essays, reviews, and memoirs have been published in the U.S. and over a dozen foreign countries. A two-time recipient of the Haiku Museum of Tokyo Award, Moore had his work included in *Haiku Moment: An Anthology of Contemporary North American Haiku.* A proud native of Jacksonville, North Carolina, he now lives in Raleigh, where he is chairman and contest coordinator of the North Carolina Haiku Society.

ARCHIBALD J. MOTLEY, JR. (1891–1981), born in New Orleans, was a graduate of The School of the Art Institute of Chicago. Motley was known for his portraiture and his careful depictions of African American nightlife and street scenes. His work has been collected by major museums and private collectors, exhibited in notable solo and group exhibitions, and was the subject of the recent retrospective *The Art of Archibald J. Motley, Jr.*

ALEXS D. PATE is a writer, poet, and performance artist living in Minneapolis. His first novel, *Losing Absalom,* won the First Novelist Award from the Black Caucus of the American Library Association and the Minnesota Book Award for 1995. He is presently at work on an anthology, *With and Without,* and a novel, *For Children with Missing Fathers.*

ELIJAH PIERCE (1892–1984), a noted woodcarver, folk artist, barber, minister, and community historian, was a keen observer of contemporary life. His woodcarvings, which include such religious masterpieces as *Book of Wood* and *Crucifixion,* as well as autobiographical, political, and sports carvings, were the subject of the 1992 retrospective *Elijah Pierce: Woodcarver,* which opened at the Columbus Museum of Art.

HORACE PIPPIN (1888–1946), born in West Chester, Pennsylvania, is regarded as among the foremost African American artists of the twentieth century, a distinction he earned despite a permanent and painful injury to his right arm sustained in World War I. Pippin first came to national attention in the 1938 Museum of Modern Art exhibition "Masters of Popular Painting," in which his paintings were shown along with those by Henri Rousseau and Edward Hicks. His works are in private collections as well as in the Philadelphia Academy of the Fine Arts, the Metropolitan Museum of Art, the Barnes Foundation, and the Art Institute of Chicago, among other museums.

ISHMAEL REED is a novelist, poet, essayist, television producer, publisher, magazine editor, playwright, radio commentator, and founder of the Before Columbus Foundation, PEN Oakland, and There City Cinema. Among his seventeen published books are the novels *Japanese by Spring* and *Reckless Eyeballing,* as well as the essay collections *Writin' is Fightin'* and *Airing Dirty Laundry.* A Oakland resident, he has most recently completed a libretto for an opera commissioned by the San Francisco Opera.

ROBERT REID was born in Atlanta and attended Clark University, The School of the Art Institute of Chicago, and the Parsons School of Design. His work has been exhibited widely in the U.S. and abroad in solo and group shows (including *Black Artists: Two Generations, Contemporary Black Artists in America,* and *Empowerment: The Art of African American Artist*) and is included in the collections of the Newark Museum of Art, the Studio Museum in Harlem, and the Museum of African Art in Washington, D.C., among others.

BETYE SAAR was born in Los Angeles, where she attended U.C.L.A. A noted master of collage and assemblage whose work exhibits strong spiritual themes, Saar has participated in over forty group and solo exhibitions in the U.S., Canada, Europe, and Asia, including *Secrets, Dialogues, Revelations,* a joint exhibit with her daughter, Alison.

ALEXANDER SMALLS is an opera singer, chef, creator of Southern Revival cooking, and owner of Café Beulah in New York City. A graduate of the Curtis Institute of Music in Philadelphia, Smalls made his Carnegie Hall debut in 1984 and has performed with Anna Moffo, Renata Scotto, Michael Tilson Thomas, and Leonard Bernstein, among others. He is currently at work on a book of recipes and reminiscences.

MARY CARTER SMITH was born in Birmingham, Alabama, and taught for thirty-one years in Baltimore's public schools. Cofounder of the National Association of Black Storytellers and the National Festival of Black Storytelling, Smith is an acclaimed storyteller and a preserver of the African oral tradition, who is considered "Mother Griot" to African American storytellers nationwide.

HENRY OSSAWA TANNER (1859–1937), the most acclaimed African American painter of the nineteenth century, was born in Pittsburgh and studied at the Pennsylvania Academy of Art with American genre painter Thomas Eakins, among others. Tanner eventually emigrated to France, where he studied and painted until his death, making only occasional visits to the United States, where he was dismayed by the racial prejudice he encountered. His religious works, begun in the mid-1890s and including such paintings as *Daniel in the Lions' Den, The Annunciation,* and *The Good Shepherd,* are in the collections of the Los Angeles County Museum of Art, the Philadelphia Museum of Art, and the National Museum of American Art, among others.

ALMA THOMAS (1896–1978), born in Columbus, Georgia, studied at Howard University, Columbia University, and American University. Thomas did not devote herself to painting full time until after her retirement from teaching in the public schools of Washington, D.C. Her first major retrospective occurred in 1966; in 1972, she was the subject of a one-woman exhibition at the Whitney Museum of American Art and the Corcoran Gallery of Art. She produced some of her most important works while in her seventies and eighties, most notably the "Earth" series and her "Space" or "Snoopy" series, the latter inspired by man's landing on the moon in 1969.

HOWARD THURMAN (1900–1981) was a distinguished philosopher, theologian, poet, and mystic. Founder of the Church for the Fellowship of All Peoples in San Francisco, the first interracial, interdenominational church in the U.S., Thurman was the author of more than twenty books, including *Meditations of the Heart, The Centering Moment, The Creative Encounter,* and *With Head and Heart,* his autobiography.

EDWARD WEBSTER was born around 1900 in Florence, South Carolina. A childhood friend of the artist William H. Johnson, Webster migrated to New York City, where he worked as a mail carrier for thirty years while he pursued his art. *The Nativity* is one of twenty-two paintings on the life of Christ that Webster painted over a twenty-year period.

JAMES L. WELLS (1902–1993) was born in Atlanta and studied at the National Academy of Design. A director of the Harlem Art Workshop and Studio and a faculty member of the Howard University School of Art, Wells was best known as a printmaker, although three of his paintings, including *Flight into Egypt,* won Harmon gold medals in fine art.

VALERIE WILSON WESLEY is editor at large at *Essence* magazine and the author of the Tamara Hayle detective series, including *When Death Comes Stealing, Devil's Gonna Get Him,* and *Where Evil Sleeps.* She is also the author of the juvenile novel *Where Do I Go From Here?,* which received an American Library Association "Best Books for Reluctant Readers" citation.

DOROTHY WEST has been heralded as one of the last remaining members of the Harlem Renaissance. She was only eighteen when her short story "The Typewriter" won the *Opportunity* magazine prize. West was a contemporary of many of the major literary figures of that era, including Wallace Thurman, Zora Neale Hurston, and Langston Hughes, and was the founder of the literary magazines *Challenge* and *New Challenge.* She is the author of two novels, *The Living is Easy* (1948) and the bestselling *The Wedding* (1994), and a collection of stories, essays, and sketches, *The Richer, The Poorer* (1995).

PAULA L. WOODS is coauthor of *I, Too, Sing America: The African-American Book of Days,* and coeditor of *I Hear a Symphony: African Americans Celebrate Love.* She is editor of *Spooks, Spies, and Private Eyes: Black Mystery, Crime, and Suspense Fiction of the 20th Century,* which was recognized by the Black Caucus of the American Library Association as an outstanding contribution to publishing. She is also cofounder of Livre Noir, a book packaging and consulting firm located in Los Angeles.